MASS KILLERS

W9-CAI-626

MASS KILLERS

Inside the Minds of Men Who Murder

David J. Krajicek

David J. Krajicek has been telling crime stories in newspapers, magazines, and books for four decades. He proudly descends from a long line of meatpackers and saloonkeepers—men and women known to tell a few stories of their own. He writes "The Justice Story," the longest-running true crime feature in American journalism, for the *New York Daily News*. The former Columbia University journalism professor is the author of eight books. A native Nebraskan, he lives in the Catskill Mountains of New York.

This edition published in 2019 by Arcturus Publishing Limited
26/27 Bickels Yard, 151–153 Bermondsey Street,
London SE1 3HA

AD006212US

Printed in the UK

Contents

Foreword 6

Introduction: Something Seriously Wrong 9

1. "Eric Harris Is God" 33

2. "You'll All Know Who I Am" 61

3. How Killers Are Made 91

4. Homicidally Horny 109

5. The "Magnificent Gentleman" 131

6. Journal of a Broken Mind 155

7. Murder in Black and White 173

8. When Slaughter Became Ordinary 197

9. The Viking King of Overkill 227

10. The Industrial Revolutionary 245

11. Die Euromörder 257

12. Twinkle Twinkle Little Gun 273

    Resources 297

    Index 301

    Picture Credits 304

Foreword

The only multiple murder I've covered was back in 1970, when *Playboy* magazine sent me out to Plainfield, Wisconsin, to try to discover why Jim McBrair, the 27-year-old son of a cucumber farmer, exploded late one afternoon and killed his wife, his wife's sister, his father-in-law, and the babysitter who was caring for his two daughters, aged five and seven. He chose not to shoot the little girls, whom he tucked safely into their beds before going to tell his father what he'd done.

The element making this a stand-out story was that McBrair exhibited none of the classic personality elements for such a demon—he wasn't a loner type, he wasn't a weirdo with loser friends, or noticeably secretive. He'd had solid Bs in high school, starred in all three seasonal sports and served as King of the junior prom.

I wrote the story after interviewing practically everyone in town, but failed to satisfy myself that I'd found the real reasons for his outburst. It emerged that he'd always held in his anger, never spoken a heated word to anyone, which is supposedly a tell-tale marker, and that he became upset upon hearing his wife was having an extra-marital affair. So, who wouldn't be? Was it then reasonable to go out and kill her and three other people?

In this remarkable book about the phenomenon of mass murder, David J. Krajicek, a former *New York Daily News* police reporter and professor at the Columbia Journalism School, has come the closest I've seen to providing helpful answers to the generally unfathomable conundrum: Why did they do it? And was it predictable what they did?

Too often, reporters searching for answers come back with a list of childhood traumas and adolescent personality traits that, as a way of explaining the roots of the latest bit of horror, seem deeply unfulfilling. They endured abuse from their fathers or schoolyard bullies, they played too much Dungeons and Dragons in the attic, they suffered from low birth weight, or had a brain tumor. Excuse me, but individuals possessing these same characteristics end up far more often leading perfectly normal lives rather than going out and suddenly shooting a lot of people.

Pulling together evidence from experts who've spent their lives studying these cases, Krajicek comes up with valuable insights that should be made available to every school counselor and teacher and child welfare worker, not to mention mothers and fathers and siblings, who might have the chance to intervene on behalf of a friend or relative before his killer instincts explode.

For one thing, he says, the signposts that should alert them to something bad coming around the bend are often plain to see: "Very few of these high-profile sprees are impulsive. Killers in this class do not 'snap.' They plan their assaults for months or even years, drawing up detailed battle plans and accumulating expensive weaponry. For many of them, documentation of this process in journals or videos is an essential component; they understand they are leaving evidence that will help the marquee lights of their crimes burn brighter and longer."

Less obvious but equally important, he writes, is that the approaching "event" creates an emotional state of mind in the killer that approaches a deep religious awakening. "Journals and videos left by many of these killers suggest burgeoning acute euphoria as the deadly date approaches, an emotional state that experts often see with suicidal people—like Christians approaching the rapture. In their minds, the path forward is finally clear. Despair is coming to an end, and a twisted form of immortality is at hand."

What's really scary about all this is the growing frequency of these mass shootings, which can lead only to more and more such incidents. As he quotes from Dr. Peter Langman, a child and adolescent psychologist who is frequently called upon by the FBI to help them find reasons for school shootings: "One way of understanding the concept of contagion is the possibility that the more the taboo against mass murder is broken, the easier it becomes for the next perpetrator. Each time that threshold is crossed may lower the threshold for people already on the path toward violence. Thus, the phenomenon may be feeding on itself, growing with each new incident." Not a comforting prospect.

Bruce Porter, author of *Blow*, *Snatched*, and *The Practice of Journalism: A Guide to Reporting and Writing the News*

Introduction: Something Seriously Wrong

10/1/18: To mark the anniversary of a terrible event, Rafael Sarabia parades the Stars and Stripes on his horse Red Sonja outside the Mandalay Bay Hotel, Las Vegas, in memory of the victims of gunman Stephen Paddock, who killed 58 people and injured 851 in the worst mass shooting in U.S. history. Paddock left no explanation for his grotesque crime.

As his craving to kill advanced from a vague fantasy to an urgent imperative, an Oregon boy named Kip Kinkel secluded himself in his bedroom one night and scrawled an 850-word primal scream in his black-jacketed journal.

> *I sit here all alone. I am always alone. I don't know who I am. I want to be something I can never be. I try so hard every day. But in the end, I hate myself for what I've become. Every single person I know means nothing to me. I hate every person on this earth. I wish they could all go away. You all make me sick. I wish I was dead . . .*
>
> *. . . I am so full of rage that I feel I could snap at any moment. I think about it every day. Blowing the school up or just taking the easy way out, and walk into a pep assembly with guns. In either case, people that are breathing will stop breathing. That is how I will repay all you motherfuckers for all you put me through. I feel like everyone is against me, but no one ever makes fun of me, mainly because they think I am a psycho. . .*
>
> *I am evil. I want to kill and give pain without a cost. And there is no such thing . . . Anyone that believes in God is a fucking sheep. If there was a God, he wouldn't let me feel the way I do. Love isn't real, only hate remains. Only hate.*

Kinkel was 15 years old when he wrote those ominous words. How does a ninth-grade child descend into such abject despair and nihilism, with a soul as leaden as the doleful, world-weary narrator in Dostoevsky's *Notes from the Underground*? "I am a sick man. I am a spiteful man. I am an unattractive man."

He explained to a psychologist that he had begun hearing voices in his head at age 12. He quoted their message: "You

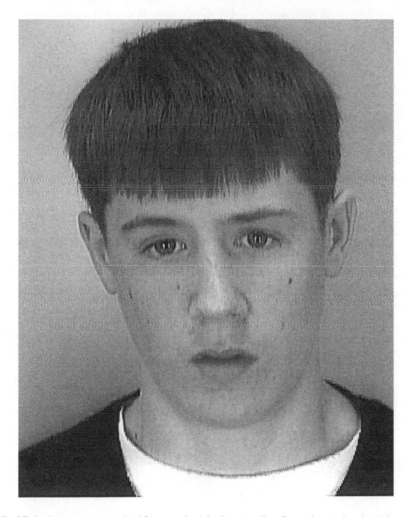

Kip Kinkel was suspended from school when police found a stolen handgun in his locker.

need to kill everyone, everyone in the world." He added: "It scared the shit out of me. I was confused. It seemed like something was seriously wrong."

Indeed, something *was* seriously wrong.

On May 20, 1998, Kinkel was suspended from school in his hometown of Springfield, Oregon, when police found a stolen handgun in his locker. That afternoon, as his father, Bill, sipped coffee at a kitchen counter after an angry exchange with his son, Kip stalked up and shot him in the back of the head with a Ruger rifle. When his mother, Faith, arrived home a few hours later, Kip met her in the garage and shot her six times—twice in the back of the head, three times in the face, and once in the heart. (He would later claim that he first expressed his love for her; she wasn't available to confirm that stirring detail.) Afterward, Kip sat down and wrote another note:

> *I have just killed my parents! I don't know what is happening. I love my mom and dad so much. I just got two felonies on my record* [related to the stolen gun]. *My parents can't take that! It would destroy them. The embarrassment would be too much for them. They couldn't live with themselves. I'm so sorry. I am a horrible son. I wish I had been aborted. I destroy everything I touch. I can't eat. I can't sleep. I didn't deserve them. They were wonderful people. It's not their fault or the fault of any person, organization, or television show. My head just doesn't work right. God damn these VOICES inside my head. I want to die. I want to be gone. But I have*

to kill people. I don't know why. I am so sorry! Why did God do this to me. I have never been happy. I wish I was happy. I wish I made my mother proud. I am nothing! I tried so hard to find happiness. But you know me—I hate everything. I have no other choice. What have I become? I am so sorry.

The next morning, he arrived at school wearing a trench coat and armed with three guns, two knives, and more than 1,000 rounds of ammunition. He shot two people in a corridor, then moved into the cafeteria, where he sprayed four dozen rounds with his .22-caliber assault rifle before he was tackled and subdued by fellow students. Altogether, he had killed two and wounded 25 at the school.

Some mass killers seek revenge and some seek fame—or infamy, its modern synonym. Some target a group or individual while others choose victims at random—wrong place, wrong time. Some are sadists, others are simply sad. Each mass killer is one of a kind and uniquely evil, but many have common characteristics. There are psychopaths, like Eric Harris, the torchbearer of the two Columbine High School killers, whose enormous ego left no room in his psyche for empathy. Others are reacting to trauma—a fractured or abusive home life, conflict with peers, or failure at romance, like the growing club of spree killers motivated by the condition that has become known, unfortunately, as "involuntary celibacy." Still others are psychotic, with schizophrenia that is often marked by delusions and hallucinations. That group includes Seung-Hui Cho, the 2007 Virginia Tech rampage killer, who imagined himself a buddy of Vladimir Putin, bragged about a supermodel Martian girlfriend, and grandly compared himself to Moses.

Brimming with Delusions

Kip Kinkel was Cho's psychological peer. In his despairing note, the teenager wasn't wrong when he described himself as a psycho because his mind was brimming with delusions. He stored explosives under his bed in readiness for an invasion by China; he feared the onset of a plague and wished to build a secure shelter stockpiled with survival provisions; he believed that The Walt Disney Co., bent on world domination, was secretly planning to launch the "Disney Dollar," a replacement currency featuring a banknote portrait of Mickey Mouse; and he suspected the government of implanting computer chips in the craniums of citizens during MRI procedures, at the same time wondering whether these were being used to broadcast the voices in his head. He also believed that he was being relentlessly stalked by a man who lived in a trailer on his route to school.

These delusions were revealed to Dr. Orin Bolstad during forensic psychological examinations of Kinkel after his murders. But more than a year earlier another shrink, Dr. Jeffrey Hicks, noted red flags in a series of psychotherapy sessions with Kinkel. Those began after Kip had been caught shoplifting and was then arrested for throwing rocks off a highway overpass onto passing cars. Faith Kinkel told Hicks that her son was "very emotional" and had a disconcerting fascination with guns and explosives. At the same time, bizarrely enough, Bill Kinkel was buying guns for his son, including the assault rifle the boy would later use to kill his parents. Dr. Hicks wrote a prescient analysis of his new young patient: "Kip is very angry and vents this anger by antisocial acting-out and detonating explosives. He is at risk for accidentally harming himself or others with explosives. He is also high risk for continued antisocial behavior."

On September 24, 1999, four days after his 17th birthday, Kipland Philip Kinkel agreed to plead guilty to four counts of murder and 26 counts of attempted murder. In exchange, he was hoping for a merciful sentence—informed by the testimony of Dr. Bolstad and others—that might offer him a chance to live as a free man at some point, even in his dotage. Instead, Judge Jack Mattison sent him to prison for 111 years, with no possibility of parole. Two decades along, Kinkel still resides behind bars. As he approaches middle age, Kinkel's prison mugshot shows a balding man staring blankly at the camera with dull blue eyes.

Factors that Trigger Violence

This book explores the troubled minds of mass killers like Kinkel through their own words. I do not regard the Oregonian or any of the others as a victim. The victims are the boys, girls, men, and women that these broken human beings killed, maimed, or otherwise wounded. And the victimization spreads in all directions from those bodies, like ripples on a pond, to include loved ones left to deal with the carnage, the mortified schoolchildren, the ruined businesses, the cities around the world riven by place-name association with these ghastly acts—Dunblane, Scotland; Port Arthur, Tasmania; Littleton, Colorado; Winnenden, Germany;

Oslo, Norway; Newtown, Connecticut; Parkland, Florida; and so many others. Pittsburgh, Pennsylvania, became a dot on this dreadful map on October 27, 2018, when an inflamed middle-aged man stormed a synagogue there and wielded an assault rifle and three pistols to kill 11 people because, as he bellowed, "All Jews must die!" These sorts of mass killings represent a small percentage of murder overall—just one or two percent. But the worst examples, including Pittsburgh, are like a catastrophic hurricane: rare, but terrifying and unforgettable.

The events in these cursed places remind us of the particular horror that accompanies random violence. Some years ago, before the Columbine High School shootings in 1999, I asked a United States federal law enforcement official how he felt about the widespread availability to the American public of the same assault rifles that soldiers use as weapons of war. His reply surprised me. He said, in essence, why should law-abiders be denied any gun because gang-bangers are using it to kill one another? It's true that many criminals knowingly engage in a lifestyle that comes with risks. But times have changed. Assault rifles have now been used on mall shoppers, classrooms of first-graders, moviegoers, country music crowds. Do we blame the first-graders for putting themselves at risk by attending school, or a collection of Coloradans for placing themselves in someone's rifle sights because they wanted to see the new Batman film? That is the terror of today's mass shootings: It seems it could happen to you, to me, to any of us—at any time.

And what well does all this violence spring from? Is it global seepage of the Yankee propensity for rogue outbursts—

described poetically by the writer Philip Roth as "the indigenous American berserk?" My examination finds three factors in nearly all headline-grabbing cases: mental illness, too-easy access to firearms (especially assault rifles), and missed signals by parents, law enforcers, school officials, or other authority figures. Elizabeth Yardley, a criminology professor at Birmingham City University in England, whose work explores the minds of murderers, tweeted a brilliantly terse analysis that goes a level deeper:

> *Mass killers, 5 commonalities: 1) History of failure, inability to cope w/ probs; 2) Blame others for it, want revenge; 3) Isolate themselves from social support; 4) Catastrophize a recent event; 5) Have access to weapon they consider apt for revenge.*

Kinkel, a contemporary school-shooting prototype, ticked all of those boxes. His family had a multi-generational history of mental illness on both sides, including schizophrenia and both homicidal and suicidal behavior, yet his parents apparently did not reveal this obviously pertinent detail as their adolescent son was being treated for acute depression. While his mother was mortified over Kip's obsession with firearms and explosives, his father was buying him deadly weapons in what seemed to be an act of wrong-headed appeasement of a difficult child. His shrink accurately predicted Kip's future violence but suspended psychotherapy when Prozac seemed to ease his depression. School officials could have treated more seriously a series of minor violent incidents by Kinkel before the shootings. And the police probably made a poor decision by releasing the boy to his father just hours after the precipitating stolen gun incident at school.

If only someone had seen the despair and kill-'em-all rhetoric in Kinkel's journal, his personal manifesto. That word, derived from the Latin *manifestus*, meaning "obvious," suggests a clear public declaration of one's beliefs, plans, or motivations.

Killers' Explanations

I have read the leavings of some 50 killers in researching this book. Some are humble, some grandiose—from brief, introspective suicide notes to tome-like whines by sex-deprived men. A few left notes and journals that are poignant while others are bloviated and reek of narcissism—fabulously egocentric, like the ultimate selfie. They range in length from an eerie, five-word message left by a Michigan school bomber nearly a century ago—"Criminals are made, not born"—to the *Mein Kampf*-sized manifesto of Norwegian mass killer Anders Breivik, whose turgid dissertation goose-steps along for nearly a million words. Not surprisingly, today, more and more mass killers choose to leave their messages on YouTube, Facebook, or some other expedient, phone-in-hand platform. (If Martin Luther were posting his *Ninety-Five Theses* now, he might spare a nail hole in the door of Wittenberg's All Saints' Church and opt for a social media blast.)

An enterprising new analysis of the language used in mass killers' explanations found clear patterns. For her doctoral dissertation, Laura E. Hamlett of Walden University studied the words of 12 killers, including Kinkel and the Columbiners.

She concluded: "My results confirmed that mass murderers' communications display common psycholinguistic themes, specifically ego survival and revenge, pseudocommando mindset, nihilism, entitlement, and heroic revenge fantasy."

Very few of these high-casualty sprees are impulsive. Killers in this class do not "snap." They plan their assaults for months or even years, drawing up detailed battle plans and accumulating expensive weaponry. For many of them, documentation of this process in journals or videos is an essential component; they understand they are leaving evidence that will help the marquee lights of their crimes burn brighter and longer.

Some of the leavings I studied merely hint at violence, but many expressly threaten mass murder, sometimes spelling out where, when, and how. During the planning process, most killers-to-be leave angry, sneering messages, though a few apologize—or express some form of regret to loved ones left behind. Some young killers have even used final notes to romantically stage-manage their own funerals. One extreme example was Jaylen Fryberg, a 15-year-old Native American—despairing over a broken romance—who killed four friends and himself in 2014 at his school near Seattle, Washington. Just before the shooting, he sent a long text message to his parents with the subject "My Funeral Shit." Among his directions:

> *I want to be fully dressed in camo in my casket. Brand new expensive-as-shit camo . . . Put my hat with the S on it on me in my casket. Put an insulin bag in my casket with me and burn one for me. I want mine, Andrews and* [name

redacted] *graves to all be lined up . . . Songs to play at my funeral. (Life style, U guessed it, hot nigga, Hookah, The Ruble by randy wood, love by Kevin Yazzie) it needs to be POPPIN! Play the randy wood and the Kevin Yazzie first and play the POPPIN SHIT next and ask* [name redacted] *for some poppin shit to play . . . I wasn't happy. And I need my crew with me too. I'm sorry. I love you.*

In many ways, Fryberg's note was a typical suicidal farewell, which one prominent American psychologist describes as "a harsh word, an apology, an explanation, or just a to-do list."

Strangely, as we will see, an increasing number of mass killers seem to treat their end-of-life journal entries as though they were dating profiles, including lists of favorite movies and music—even colors and snacks. For some of these murderers, nothing about themselves is too granular or extraneous to leave out. At three in the morning on September 4, 2006, nine days before he shot 20 students at Dawson College in Montreal, Canada, Kimveer Gill posted this entry in his online journal: "I ate some cheesy poofs. Ya know, those cheese stick things, like Cheetos. Ahhhhhh, now you see. The power of the cheesy poof cannot be denied." A few days later, he had regressed from snack-happy to Mr. Pitiful. He wrote: "Fuck people. Fuck life. Fuck god."

Many close observers of these cases believe that we—collectively, the mass media and the rubbernecking public—indulge these fractured, needy individuals when we look to their leavings for deep thoughts that, in most cases, don't exist. "Our collective fascination with bizarre crimes—cleverly repackaged as a desire to understand aberrant behavior—has us as a willing audience for all sorts of violent malcontents," says James Alan Fox, an eminent American criminologist. "But we must avoid lending any credibility to such rants and raves." Fox was particularly nettled by the voluminous record left behind by Elliot Rodger, the self-proclaimed "magnificent gentleman" who killed six people and injured 14 others near UC Santa Barbara, California in 2014. Fox wrote:

> *Why would this young man devote so much time and energy to reporting on his pitiful existence? Why would he then publicly distribute a document that hardly portrays him in a positive light?*
>
> *Like many other rampage killers before him, Rodger likely felt the need to set the record straight—to inform the world about his justification for carnage. He may have reasoned that without his written words and recorded explanation, society would conclude he was just some deranged individual who suddenly snapped and slaughtered innocent victims for no reason at all. It would have been important for Rodger to demonstrate that at the end of the day, despite the history of bullying and social ostracism, he emerged victorious. He apparently wanted us to know that he was the good guy, not the evil one, who was ready to exact retribution for the injustices he had endured and ultimately to win one for, quite literally, the little guy.*

Of course, our species harbors an enduring and deep fascination with murder and murderers. Perhaps owing to some primordial survival instinct, we seek clues to both the killer's motivations and the circumstances that drew a victim into his orbit. And on a more superficial level, mass killings are like an automobile wreck—or a hurricane. How can we not look?

Most Killers Are Male

Like Rodger, Gill, and Kinkel, nearly all mass killers are male. In the U.S., about one in ten are female. Just one woman turns up on the list of the 27 deadliest shootings in U.S. history: Tashfeen Malik, who with her husband, Syed Rizwan Farook, killed 14 and wounded 22 others in a 2015 terrorist attack in San Bernardino, California. Those perpetrators stood out in ethnicity, as well. About six out of every ten mass killers are white. The German writer Hans Magnus Enzensberger has suggested that mass killers (including terrorists) ought to be regarded as "radical losers," suicidal men who seek to bring the world down around them as they end their own lives. He explained in *Der Spiegel* in 2006:

> *This is the only solution to his problem that he can imagine: a worsening of the evil conditions under which he suffers. The newspapers run stories on him every week: the father of two who killed his wife, his small children, and finally himself. Unthinkable! A headline in the local section: A Family Tragedy. Or the man who suddenly barricades himself in his apartment, taking the landlord, who wanted money from him, as his hostage. When the*

police finally arrive on the scene, he starts shooting. Then he is said to run "amok," in the original Malay sense of the word. He kills an officer before collapsing in a shower of bullets. What triggered this explosion remains unclear. His wife's nagging perhaps, noisy neighbors, an argument in a bar, or the bank canceling his loan. A disparaging remark from a superior is enough to make the man climb a tower and start firing at anything that moves outside the supermarket, not in spite of but precisely because of the fact that this massacre will accelerate his own end. Where on earth did he get that submachine gun? At last, this radical loser—he may be just fifteen and having a hard time with his acne—at last, he is master over life and death. Then, in the newsreader's words, he "dies at his own hands" and the investigators get down to work. They find a few videos, a few confused journal entries. The parents, neighbors, teachers noticed nothing unusual. A few bad grades, for sure, a certain reticence—the boy did not talk much. But that is no reason to shoot dead a dozen of his schoolmates. The experts deliver their verdicts. Cultural critics bring forth their arguments. Inevitably, they speak of a "debate on values." The search for reasons comes to nothing. Politicians express their dismay. The conclusion is reached that it was an isolated case.

That may seem cynical, but do insights emerge from this apparently seamless series of "isolated" cases? Suicide notes, journals, and manifestos offer far more information and context than the standard interview-the-neighbors profiles slapped together by generations of journalists covering calamitous violent crimes. On the other hand, how much do we really learn while trying to peer into these dark souls? As Columbine's Harris astutely noted: "Sometimes we will spend an entire lifetime trying to figure out someone, and even after that length of time we still can't possibly know everything about that person. The same goes for ourselves." Those words surely resonated with the mother of Harris's killing partner, Dylan Klebold. A central theme of Sue Klebold's memoir was the shocking realization that the stranger she feared most proved to be the fruit of her own womb.

Yet essential contours come into relief in what Enzensberger called "confused journal entries," which may help unravel the mysteries of what experts view as a mass shooting contagion in the U.S., Canada, Germany, and, to a lesser degree, Scandinavia and other European precincts. (To be clear: As we shall see, mass murders happen in other countries, but the U.S. is far and away the worldwide leader.) "The phenomenon is feeding on itself," warns Peter Langman, a Pennsylvania psychologist who is the world's premier researcher of school shootings. (He generously shares his analyses and archive at SchoolShooters. info.) Few doubt that *something* is prompting a surge in mass shootings that began in the early 1980s. But what?

Killers Rarely Survive

Here's one clue: It has become increasingly rare for spree killers to survive. Three-quarters of the men on the list of the highest-casualty American mass murderers died during the events. About half committed suicide, and others were killed by law enforcers, often as part of the plan. Journals and videos left by many of these killers suggest burgeoning acute euphoria as the deadly date approached, an emotional state that experts often see with suicidal people—like Christians approaching the rapture. In their minds, the path forward is finally clear. Despair is coming to an end, and a twisted form of immortality is at hand. They masquerade their "true depressive despair," according to Henry J. Friedman, a Harvard psychiatry professor, amid their "desire to end life early surrounded by an aurora of apocalyptic destruction."

Many of these killers feel compelled to point out in their final notes that they are not insane—sometimes using the legalese "of sound mind and body"—despite all evidence to the contrary. ("I WILL be armed to the fuckin teeth and i WILL shoot to kill and i WILL fucking KILL EVERYTHING!" Eric Harris wrote online. "No i am not crazy. Crazy is just a word. To me it has no meaning. Everyone is different.") Suicide experts disagree with the killer's self-analysis. They say mental issues—such things as depression, bipolar disorder, and schizophrenia—underlie as many as nine out of every ten suicides. Edwin Shneidman, the late California psychologist and leading suicide researcher, coined the word "psychache" to describe the "unbearable psychological pain" of suicidal people.

Karin Andriolo, an anthropology professor in New Paltz, New York, says these "masked suicides . . . illuminate how suicide by mass murder can be an instrumental way of living up to cultural ideals for those who feel marginalized." In other words, suicide as much as murder is the intent of the killers. Another pair of State University of New York researchers, Rachel Kalish and Michael Kimmel, link school shootings to the sense of gender entitlement of "toxic masculinity." In a 2010 journal article entitled "Suicide by Mass Murder," they wrote:

> . . . *as media portrayals of these "rampages" shock the public, the characterization of this violence obscures an important point: many of these crimes culminate in suicide, and they are almost universally committed by males. We examine three recent American cases, which involve suicide, to elucidate how the culture of hegemonic masculinity in the U.S. creates a sense of aggrieved entitlement conducive to violence. This sense of entitlement simultaneously frames suicide as an appropriate, instrumental behavior for these males to underscore their violent enactment of masculinity.*

Misogyny, misanthropy, and racism are threads that bind together many of the men and boys profiled in this book. Although females were not the primary targets of their enmity, Norway's Breivik and Ted Kaczynski, the American Unabomber, went off on manifesto tangents about feminist women, whom they regarded as hypersensitive and "politically correct."

"This is payback," Columbiner Harris replied to a girl who asked why he was shooting his classmates. "This is what you deserve."

Shortly before shooting 32 people at Virginia Tech, Seung-Hui Cho glared at a video camera and growled: "Are you happy now that you have destroyed my life?"

"Tell me, was it worth it?" George Hennard asked repeatedly in 1991, as he singled out women while shooting 50 people at a Lubbock, Texas, cafeteria, killing 23. Most mass killers exhibit what Kalish and Kimmel call "a self-justifying sense of righteousness to their actions." The researchers added:

> *What transforms the aggrieved into mass murderers is also a sense of entitlement, a sense of using violence against others, making others hurt as you, yourself, might. Aggrieved entitlement inspires revenge against those who have wronged you; it is the compensation for humiliation. Humiliation is emasculation: humiliate someone and you take away his manhood. For many men, humiliation must be avenged, or you cease to be a man. Aggrieved entitlement is a gendered emotion, a fusion of that humiliating loss of manhood and the moral obligation and entitlement to get it back. And its gender is masculine.*

Tradition of Suicide Notes

People have been killing themselves—and leaving suicide notes—since ancient times. (Fortunately, most go unaccompanied into the hereafter.) One-quarter to one-third of all men and women who commit suicide leave some form of farewell or explanation. That's a lot of paper: In the U.S. alone, about 125 people kill themselves every single day—which is about 45,000 each year, nearly triple the number of annual homicides in the U.S. American males kill themselves three times more frequently than females—roughly 35,000 men and boys commit suicide compared with 10,000 women and girls per annum. That disparity helps explain the vast gender gap among mass killers. Suicide rates in the U.S. have increased by about 30 percent in the new millennium while declining about 20 percent in Western Europe.

The first record we have of a man's thoughts while approaching suicide—believed to have been written in Egypt in about 2100 BC—shares themes in notes left by contemporary mass killers. The unnamed Egyptian's note, discovered more than a century ago, was a vast undertaking, with a narrative section and a series of poems. Dr. Chris Thomas, a Leicester, England, psychiatrist who wrote about the document in the *British Medical Journal*, diagnosed the writer as "severely psychotically depressed . . . with feelings of persecution and self-depreciation." In the narrative, a man who views himself as poor, friendless, and shamed by society commits to suicide by self-immolation. His poems describe his misery, born of shame and isolation. A few excerpts:

> *Lo, my name is abhorred,*
> *Lo, more than the odor of carrion*
> *On days in summer, when the sky is hot . . .*

> *Lo, my name is abhorred,*
> *Lo, more than that of a wife*
> *When lies are told against her to her husband . . .*

To whom do I speak today?
I am laden with misery,
And lack a trusty friend . . .

In his final poems, he is uplifted by the approach of death—
suicidal euphoria?—and looks forward to a godlike existence for
eternity, again like many contemporary mass killers. There are
hints of revenge, as well:

Death is before me today
As when a man longs to see his house again,
After he has spent many years in captivity . . .

He that is yonder will be
One as a living god,
And will inflict punishment for sin on him that does it.

He that is yonder will be
One that stands in the sun's ship,
And will therein assign the choicest things unto the temples.

In Western culture, the romance of end-of-life notes emerged
after the publication of Goethe's *The Sorrows of Young Werther*
in 1774. The sensitive and suicidal protagonist, caught in an
unresolvable love triangle, penned an auf Wiedersehen then shot
himself in the head, prompting a real-life surge in both suicides
and explanatory notes. Eric Harris has become the Young
Werther to mass killers, particularly those who choose schools

as their venue of death. Manifestos of murder were rare before his 1999 Columbine spree. We now presume that mass killers will leave an explanation, and it becomes news when they don't. Stephen Paddock, the suicidal Baby Boomer who killed a record 58 people attending a music festival in Las Vegas in 2017, was an outlier because he was determinedly mute about his motivations.

By contrast, the Columbiners' trove is easily accessed on the Internet, and several dozen derivative killers in the U.S. and abroad have culled and copied details pioneered by Harris and Klebold, as we'll see in the next chapter. Just as 18th century lovelorn souls were inspired by Werther, today's alienated young men identify with Harris, who spewed macho declarations that made his guns seem like penile extenders. These radical losers, many of them enthralled by military might and weapons of war, reckon that they are joining an eternal club of fist-bumping pseudocommandos. In their minds, they set themselves apart when they commit the godly act of ending lives—a hypermasculine sadism that often masks deep psychological insecurities, including damaged masculinity. Erich Fromm, the late psychoanalysis pathfinder, said sadists need "the sensation of controlling and choking life." He wrote:

> *He is sadistic because he feels impotent, unalive, and powerless. He tries to compensate for this lack by having power over others, by transforming the worm he feels himself to be into a god. But even the sadist who has power suffers from his human impotence. He may kill and torture, but he remains a loveless, isolated, frightened person . . .*

Inevitability of Mass Murder

Many mass killers have declared themselves part of an imaginary revolution—a "war of vendetta," the Virginia Tech mass shooter called it. The idea that these aggrieved males are world-changing revolutionaries might seem patently absurd, as it did to me when I began to study their macho rhetoric. But if the endgame of the revolution is repeated examples of mass murder, haven't they succeeded in a sense—over and over again?

News stories of mass shootings often feature the same two or three adjectives—unthinkable, senseless, random. It seems to me that inevitable is a much more accurate adjective. Sigmund Freud noted that the need to remind people that "thou shall not kill," a rule spelled out in the sacred texts of most faiths, "makes it certain that we are descended from an endlessly long chain of generations of murderers, whose love of murder was in their blood as it is perhaps also in ours."

The snowballing contagion of mass shootings has several facets of inevitability. For one, the death count of today's mass killing becomes a target for tomorrow's perpetrator—a subject that has come up repeatedly in manifestos since Columbine. The contagion also normalizes mass murder until we shrug at what once was "unthinkable."

I believe the 2012 elementary school shooting in Newtown, Connecticut was a what's-the-use moment for many Americans. If the United States federal government—bound and gagged by politicians in the thrall of pro-gun enterprises—could not be motivated to act on the murder of first-graders, then nothing will.

"One way of understanding the concept of contagion is the possibility that the more the taboo against mass murder is broken, the easier it becomes for the next perpetrator," Peter Langman, the school shooting expert, writes. "Each time that threshold is crossed may lower the threshold for people already on the path toward violence. Thus, the phenomenon may be feeding on itself, growing with each new incident."

The message is foreboding, unfortunately.

Chapter 1.
"Eric Harris Is God"

At 11:10 a.m. on April 20, 1999, two senior students, Eric Harris and Dylan Klebold, drove separately to Columbine High School, in the Denver, Colorado, suburb of Littleton, carrying guns and bombs. On their way they placed a fire bomb in a field, about three miles away from the school. The intention was to draw firefighters, police, and others away from Columbine High, so they could go about their planned attack unhindered.

Their first stop was the cafeteria, where they planted two 20-pound propane bombs in duffel bags, set to go off at 11:17. They intended to sit outside until the bombs exploded, and then shoot anybody who managed to hightail it out of the inferno. But when the devices turned out to be duds, they hastily adapted their strategy and began walking toward the school entrance.

It was a warm day, so a number of kids were sitting outside the cafeteria. As they walked, the two trench-coated assassins shot their fellow students indiscriminately, while throwing pipe bombs. Once inside the school, they made their way to the library, shooting at students and staff, and throwing bombs, as they went. A bunch of students tried to shelter under the library desks but the shooters just fired over and under their victims' flimsy hiding places, while constantly taunting them. At one point, Harris yelled: "Who's ready to die next?" All the time they were shooting they laughed and hollered, like they were having a ball. Ten students died in the library and 12 were injured.

By the time Harris and Klebold turned their guns on themselves, at 12:08, 12 students and a teacher had died, and 24 others were wounded, some of them critically.

Although the incident shocked America from coast to coast, and sparked a national debate about gun control and security in schools, Harris and Klebold's original plan was to blow up the whole school. If the two 20-pound propane bombs they left in the cafeteria had detonated, most of the 500 or so students having lunch would have been killed, and the library above might have come crashing down.

Their cars were also filled with propane explosives, which they intended to drive into the crowds of rescuers and journalists in the wake of the blast.

The Eric Harris Brand

If mass murder by violently angry white teenagers is indeed a contagion, then Eric David Harris is the Typhoid Mary of this particular disease. In death, the alpha of the two Columbine High School killers has become a totem for a peer group of defeated souls, and his name would rest at the pinnacle of an organizational chart of the world's mass killers from the past two

Eric Harris (left) and Dylan Klebold captured on CCTV during their killing spree at Columbine High on April 20, 1999, when 13 people died.

decades. The journal and videos he left behind have helped create a lingua franca for sociopathic fanboys around the globe. His words and phrases have created an Eric Harris brand, and they turn up repeatedly in the journals, suicide notes, and social media posts of young acolytes: *Ich bin gott. Natural Selection. Kickstart a revolution. Natural Born Killer. Wrath. I'm full of hate and I love it.*

"ERIC HARRIS IS GOD!" a German teenager named Sebastian Bosse wrote in his journal in 2006, four weeks before attacking a school. "There is no doubt." And before his knife attack on a Pennsylvania school in 2014, Alex Hribal wrote: "I became a prophet because I spread the word of a god, Eric

Harris." Randy Stair, a Pennsylvania mass shooter three years later, wrote, "I love you, Eric Harris, you da man!" And Aaron Ybarra, who shot up a college campus in Washington state in 2014, described Harris as "a master of all shooters." (Scores of fangirls around the world have also paid romantic homage to Harris in blogs and on social media. "I'm in love with a dead school shooter," chirped one.)

Psychologist Langman has created the most complete record of the web of interconnections among these killers, and he places Harris at its center. He has linked Harris to nearly 35 school shooters from the U.S., Brazil, Canada, Finland, and Germany, who have quoted Harris, expressed their admiration, and copied his clothing, weapons, slogans, and techniques. The tally includes names that are both obscure and familiar: Pekka-Eric Auvinen, Alvaro Castillo, Virginia Tech killer Cho, Vester Flanagan, Kimveer Gill, Chris Harper-Mercer, Tim Kretschmer, Adam Lanza, Matti Saari, Robert Steinhäuser, and Jeffrey Weise, among others. "It is their way of joining a subculture in which they are not only normal," Langman writes, "but perhaps feel themselves to be special, apart from and above mainstream society."

The depth of this tribalism is spotlighted in a quip that Lanza made online in 2011, a year before he launched his shocking attack on a Connecticut elementary school. "Serial killers are lame," Lanza wrote. "Everyone knows that mass murderers are the cool kids." And Cho, the Virginia Tech mass killer, painted a disturbing, dystopian word picture of this murderous horde in his own pre-mortem messages:

The vendetta you have witnessed today will reverberate throughout every home and every soul in America and will inspire the innocent kids that you have fucked to start a war of vendetta. We will raise hell on earth that the world has never witnessed. Millions of deaths and millions of gallons of blood on the streets will not quench the avenging phoenix that you have caused us to unleash. Generation after generation, we martyrs, like Eric and Dylan, will sacrifice our lives to fuck you thousandfold for what you Apostles of Sin have done to us.

In his own journal, Harper-Mercer, who killed nine people on an Oregon college campus in 2015, placed himself in the "elite" pantheon of mass killers—"people who stand with the gods," including "the Columbine kids." In this chilling passage, Harper-Mercer tried to rally like-minded outsiders to join the bloody continuum:

And just like me, there will be others, like Ted Bundy said, we are your sons, your brothers, we are everywhere. My advice to others like me is to buy a gun and start killing people. If you live in a country like Europe [sic] *with strict gun laws, either pay the necessary fees/time to get a license or become a serial killer. The world could always use an additional serial killer. Butcher them in their homes, in the street, wherever you find them . . . Human life means nothing, we are what matters. I hope to inspire the masses with this, at least enough to get their passions aroused. It is my hope that others will hear my call and act it out. I was once like you, a loser, rejected by society.*

It might seem like juvenile bluster or fantasy ideology—except that these writers became killers. They *believed* they were part of a movement and drew motivation and comfort from that collective. Standing at the center of the bloodshed is a formerly obscure and frail-looking kid from the Denver suburb of Littleton, Colorado. Although modestly popular in high school, Harris was apoplectic about the exalted status of athletes and preppies and, like nearly all needy adolescents, chagrined at his own shortcomings.

Pre-Columbine Shootings

How did Harris become a mythological figure in this cult of crime celebrity? The scope of his attack was one factor. Harris and his beta partner, Dylan Klebold, using a mind-numbing array of guns and explosives that they had manufactured and stored under their parents' noses. Their reputations were further burnished by the finality of the attack—their suicides. But Harris attained transcendent status because he presciently spoke directly to a cohort whose existence he had sensed based upon a cluster of earlier shootings by young men and boys. He declared Columbine a revolutionary battlefront in the video "basement tapes" that he and Klebold recorded in the weeks before their 1999 massacre and spoke at the same time to both future victims and future disciples.

Harris: You guys will all die, and it will be fucking soon!
I hope you get an idea of what we're implying here. You
all need to die! We need to die, too! We need to fucking
kick-start the revolution here!
Klebold: The most deaths in U.S. history.
Harris (kissing his shotgun): Hopefully.

The world was agape at the security-camera images of two alienated teenagers with assault rifles stalking their high school corridors and picking off defenseless classmates over seemingly picayune beefs. But they had immediate antecedents, showing that a cauldron of violence among disturbed adolescent boys was already on the boil, because seven separate school-linked shootings had occurred in the U.S. over the previous two years. On February 2, 1996, Barry Loukaitis, 14, used his father's hunting rifle and handguns to kill a teacher and two students at his Moses Lake, Washington, middle school. A year later, on February 19, 1997, Evan Ramsey, 16, shot and killed a classmate and the principal at his school in Bethel, Alaska. Then on October 1 of that same year Luke Woodham, 16, stabbed and bludgeoned his mother to death at home before killing two classmates—one of them a former girlfriend—at his Pearl, Mississippi, school. Two months later, on December 1, Michael Carneal,14, killed three classmates and wounded five others in West Paducah, Kentucky.

The shooting-age threshold descended further on March 24, 1998, when Mitchell Johnson, 13, and Andrew Golden, 11, used guns stolen from a relative to kill five and wound ten at their school near Jonesboro, Arkansas. A month later, on April 24, 1998, Andrew Wurst, 14, killed one and wounded three at a school dance in Edinboro, Pennsylvania. Kip Kinkel's murder of his parents and two classmates in Springfield, Oregon, came on May 20 that year.

These were not a geographical cluster. Six of the murders were spread over a 2,500-mile (4,000 km) swath of the contiguous United States, from the Southeast to the Northwest regions, and the seventh was in a remote corner of Alaska accessible only by water or air. Yet the shootings had commonalities, beginning with a school connection and the adolescence of the perpetrators. Most occurred in rural areas or smaller cities and although several apparently had planned suicide, all of the shooters survived and faced criminal justice consequences. Journalists, investigators, and shrinks scoured their oral and written records for clues of impending violence.

Several of these cases prompted a focus on the killers' histories with violent films, games, books, and pornography—a disputable pursuit that continues today, touted by President Donald Trump after the 2018 school shootings, though many see that strategy as a calculated feint away from a more obvious factor: access to guns. Beyond the firearms connection, each case featured a perpetrator filled with existential rage who viewed himself as lonely, disaffected, and somehow set-upon by the world.

As Langman wrote:

These were young men who were raging against the conditions of their existence. They were not just angry

with a person or a group of people . . . It was rage
against a world that was unfair and incomprehensible.
(They) realized they were misfits . . . They struggled
socially and felt isolated. They raged against the
cruelty of fate that they were born impaired and could
never be like other people.

Proclamations of Sanity

Kip Kinkel, raised by loving schoolteacher parents in Oregon, is the 15-year-old who left a stream of numbing nihilism in his journal: "I hate myself . . . You all make me sick . . . I wish I was dead . . . I hate living." And Luke Woodham, the young Mississippi killer, left a distinctively raging manifesto. In one sickening entry, written 24 months before his attack, he described "my first kill," when he and a friend clubbed, tortured, burned, and drowned "my dear dog Sparkle."

"I will never forget the howl she made," he wrote. "It sounded almost human. We laughed and hit her hard." Woodham tried to explain his wrath in a note written shortly before he acted it out:

I am not insane! I am angry. This world has shit on me
for the final time. I am not spoiled or lazy, for murder is
not weak and slow-witted, murder is gutsy and daring.
I killed because people like me are mistreated every
day. I did this to show society "push us and we will push
back!" I suffered all my life. No one ever truly loved me.

No one ever truly cared about me . . . And all throughout
my life I was ridiculed. Always beaten, always hated . . .
But I shall tell you one thing, I am malicious because
I am miserable. The world has beaten me. Wednesday,
[October] 1, 1997, shall go down in history as the day I
fought back.

Woodham was another of the many young mass killers who have
felt compelled to proclaim their sanity, but Michael Slobodian, a
suicidal 16-year-old school shooter who killed two and wounded
13 in 1975 in Ontario, Canada, was an early adopter. "I am not
insane," Slobodian wrote, "but just strictly fed up with life. I am
not getting myself anywhere, and it's my fault." Finland's Auvinen
left a similar dead-end message, writing: "You will probably say
to me that I am 'insane,' 'crazy,' 'psychopath,' 'criminal,' or crap
like that. No, the truth is that I am just an animal . . . I have
had enough." Dylann Roof, the South Carolina church shooter
motivated by racism, also proclaimed, "I am not crazy," but said
it as he stood firing at his victims. He did so for a reason, whether
he knew it or not. Experts suggest that Roof and the others likely
were trying to convince themselves. In their minds, insanity
would negate the legitimacy and rationale of their actions. For
that same reason, Roof refused an insanity defense at his trial.

As with so many elements of contemporary school
shootings, Eric Harris became a trend leader when he wrote on
his website: "No I am not crazy . . . Crazy is just a word." In his
videotapes, Harris insisted that he and Klebold deserved credit
as founders of their bleak revolution. "Do not think we're trying

to copy anyone," Harris said. "We had the idea before the first one ever happened. Our plan is better, not like those fucks in Kentucky with camouflage and .22s."

The Trench Coat Mafia

The Columbiners are credited with inspiring the preferred couture of young mass shooters by labeling themselves the "Trench Coat Mafia" and posing for selfies wearing backward baseball caps and black duster-style trench coats. But they surely noticed that in the earlier shootings Washington's Loukaitis wore a western-style black duster and Alaska's Ramsey wore a trench coat. And before Harris made headlines, the special brand of sociopathy exhibited by Woodham, Kinkel, and others in the late-1990s shooting cluster had already suggested a contagion. As author Malcolm Gladwell described it: "The problem is not that there is an endless supply of deeply disturbed young men who are willing to contemplate horrific acts. It's worse. It's that young men no longer need to be deeply disturbed to contemplate horrific acts."

The Columbine killers began attracting dreamy admirers within a month of their attack and suicides. On May 20, 1999, T.J. Solomon, 15 years old, used his stepfather's .22-caliber rifle to shoot up his high school east of Atlanta in Conyers, Georgia. He wounded six students but failed to kill anyone. (A .22 can be deadly, but the small-bore varmint rifle is less lethal than an assault rifle built for warfare.) During Solomon's criminal trial for aggravated assault, his prosecutor argued: "Columbine was the trigger that gave T.J. the permission to do it. It showed a way that T.J. could gain power. He could be in control. He envisioned he could be someone—that he could be infamous."

Solomon himself admitted that Columbine was a central inspiration. He left a note before the shooting that mentioned his "brothers and sisters in the trench coat mafia." And he had hinted at his intention to follow in Harris's footsteps during a discussion of Columbine at a Boy Scout meeting. "I should do something like that" to "jocks and preps," he said. "It should have happened to our school a long time ago." After the shooting, police said Solomon "emphasized how much he envied the attention that the Columbine killers got as a result of their deeds." Solomon was convicted and spent 17 years locked up before he was paroled in 2016.

Self-Radicalization and the Internet

While Harris and Klebold won attention based on the ferocity of their attack, they were also savvy about the media and popular culture at a moment when the Internet was transforming interpersonal communication. Harris, an A student who could be charming, understood the potential. "Maybe we will even start a little rebellion or revolution to fuck things up as much as we can," he wrote in his 16-page journal, which he entitled "The Book of God." "I want to leave a lasting impression on the world."

Ejaculating teenage machismo, the pair ranted racist screeds on their videos, singling out blacks, Hispanics, and Jews while adding that they hated every race, including "fucking whites." Like many young white mass murderers, Harris professed to admire Adolf Hitler, who represents unassailable power to those who feel powerless. Harris staged their attack on April 20 because it was the Führer's birthday. (In a bizarre vignette from their basement tapes, Dylan griped about his mandatory attendance at an upcoming Passover Seder, and Harris was flummoxed to learn that Klebold's mother was Jewish.)

Not so long ago, an anti-Semitic teenager might have huddled under the blankets with a copy of *The Protocols of the Elders of Zion*, but research is easier today. A Jew-obsessed youth can find voluminous materials about Harris's thoughts on Hitler and Germany; his journal is pocked with phrases in the German language. Beyond that, the sheriff's report on the case, which surpasses 25,000 pages, is available online. When we add to that a total of perhaps 25 books, films, and television programs about Columbine, the body of easily accessed information about Harris is nearly endless, and that has allowed mass killer fanboys to come out from under the bed covers.

James Comey, the former FBI director, once suggested that the Internet had made it too easy for domestic terrorists to "self-radicalize." He might as well have been talking about angry young white males when he said:

> *Because the Internet offers the ability for people to consume poison and radicalize entirely in private, either through a device they are holding in their hand or inside their house, our visibility is necessarily limited. And so we constantly worry . . . about who is out there on this journey from consuming poison to acting on it and can we get eyes on them in time to stop it.*

Tortured Journals of the Columbiners

Harris and Klebold fed off one another, as well. Some shrinks have cited the pair as an example of delusion by proxy—or *folie à deux*—where a dominant figure (Harris) foists his psychosis on a subordinate (Klebold). In an introduction to *A Mother's Reckoning*, Sue Klebold's memoir about her son, Columbia University psychology professor Andrew Solomon suggested that Harris was a stone-cold killer. But he compared his partner to the twitchy protagonist of J.D. Salinger's *The Catcher in the Rye*. "Eric Harris was a failed Hitler; Dylan was a failed Holden Caulfield," Solomon wrote. He continued:

> *Eric Harris appears to have been a homicidal psychopath, and Dylan Klebold, a suicidal depressive, and their disparate madnesses were each other's necessary condition. Dylan's depressiveness would not have turned into murderousness without Harris' leadership, but something in Eric might have lost motivation without the thrill of dragging Dylan down with him. Eric's malice is shocking, Dylan's acquiescence equally so.*

Imbued with ennui, angst, and irritation, Klebold's journal shines a light on his tortured psyche, including one telling passage from 1997, a reckoning of his life in a soliloquy directed toward God:

> *Why the fuck is he being such an ASSHOLE??? (god I guess, whoever is the being which controls shit). He's fucking me over big time & it pisses me off. Oooh god I*

HATE my life, I want to die really bad right now—let's see what I have that's good: A nice family, a good house, food, a couple of good friends, & possessions. What's bad—no girls (friends or girlfriends), no other friends except a few, nobody accepting me even though I want to be accepted, me doing badly & being intimidated in any & all sports, me looking weird & acting shy—BIG problem, me getting bad grades, having no ambition of life, that's the big shit. Anyway . . .

He followed that a few months later with this charming puppy-love reverie:

Oh my God . . . I am almost sure I am in love . . . with [name redacted]. Hehehe . . . such a strange name, like mine . . . yet everything about her I love. From her good body to her almost perfect face, her charm, her wit & cunning, her NOT being popular. Her friends (who I know)—some—I just hope she likes me as much as I LOVE her. I think of her every second of every day. I want to be with her. I imagine me & her doing things together, the sound of her laugh, I picture her face, I love her. If soulmates exist, then I think I've found mine. I hope she likes Techno . . . :-)

His partner, Harris, was not inclined toward sweetness and self-reflection—let alone smiley-face emoticons. Like a textbook example of antisocial personality disorder, he could not muster empathy for anyone—the disabled, racial minorities, women.

These excerpts are from the journal he began keeping a year before his school massacre:

> *People that only know stupid facts that aren't important should be shot, what fucking use are they. NATURAL SELECTION. Kill all retards, people with brain fuck ups, drug addicts, people who can't figure out how to use a fucking lighter. Geeeawd! People spend millions of dollars on saving the lives of retards, and why. I don't buy that shit like "oh, he's my son, though!" So the fuck what, he ain't normal, kill him. Put him out of his misery.*
>
> *I feel like God and I wish I was, having everyone being OFFICIALLY lower than me. I already know that I am higher than most anyone in the fucking welt* [German for world] *in terms of universal intelligence . . .*
>
> *People always say we shouldn't be racist. Why not? Blacks ARE different. Like it or not they are. They started out on the bottom so why not keep 'em there. It took them centuries to convince us that they are equal but they still use their color as an excuse or they just discriminate us because we are white. Fuck you, we should ship yer black asses back to Afrifuckingca where you came from. We brought you here and we will take you back. America = white. Gays . . . well all gays, ALL gays, should be killed. Mit keine fragen* [without question]. *. . .*
>
> *If you recall your history the Nazis came up with a "final solution" to the Jewish problem. Kill them all. Well, in case you haven't figured it out yet, I say "KILL*

MANKIND." No one should survive . . . All you fuckers should die! DIE! . . . Fuck money fuck justice fuck morals fuck civilized fuck rules fuck laws . . .

Harris set that tone of rejecting all moral principles in the very first words of his journal: "I hate the fucking world, to[o] many god damn fuckers in it." He returned to the theme of hate again and again. Here is a series of his riffs from November 1998:

HATE! I'm full of hate and I love it. I HATE PEOPLE and they better fucking fear me if they know what's good for 'em. Yes I hate and I guess I want others to know it, yes I'm racist and I don't mind. Niggs and spics bring it on themselves, and another thing, I am very racist towards white trash P.O.S.'s [pieces of shit] . . .

I love the Nazis too . . . by the way, I fucking can't get enough of the swastika, the SS, and the iron cross. Hitler and his head boys fucked up a few times and it cost them the war, but I love their beliefs and who they were, what they did, and what they wanted . . .

Fuck fuck fuck. It'll be very fucking hard to hold out until April. If people would give me more compliments all of this might still be avoidable . . . but probably not. Whatever I do people make fun of me, and sometimes directly to my face. I'll get revenge soon enough. Fuckers shouldn't have ripped on me so much, huh? Ha!

It's clear that Harris used his obscene macho rants to obscure a fractured psyche. Aubrey Immelman, a Minnesota psychology professor, concluded after an analysis of his journal that Harris was sadistic, antisocial, and paranoid. He diagnosed "malignant narcissism," which features "extreme grandiosity and self-confidence, and self-absorption to the extent that one is incapable of empathizing with others' pain and suffering." Other experts have declared Harris a "compensatory narcissist"; that is, someone who "seek[s] to fill their sense of emptiness by creating an illusion of superiority," according to the late American psychologist Theodore Millon, a pioneering analyst of personality disorders.

Columbine-Inspired Shooters

Yet Harris's self-puffery has had lasting appeal among a cult of despairing young men who view him as an anti-hero. The homages continue, two decades later. Before he shot up his Santa Fe, Texas, high school on May 18, 2018, Dimitrios Pagourtzis, 17, donned a black duster trench coat affixed with a red star medallion like one worn by Dylan Klebold in 1999. Pagourtzis, who survived, killed two teachers and eight students.

Here are thumbnails of others who have paid homage to the Columbiners:

- Alvaro Castillo, 18, was foremost among the Columbine obsessives. Castillo accumulated a vast archive of Columbine memorabilia and convinced himself— paradoxically—that the most heavily publicized mass shooting in contemporary U.S. history had been forgotten. He even persuaded his mother to join him on a 1,700-mile (2,730 km) sojourn to Columbine in June 2006; she hoped the trip would diminish his *idée fixe*, but it did not. (He bought a Harris-inspired trench coat while in Colorado.) After the trip, he wrote: "I know that I am doing the right thing. We must remember Columbine. Sacrifices must be made."

Castillo was one of several killers to express romantic feelings for Harris, some verging on epistolary romances. He wrote in his journal: "Eric Harris is just so good-looking. I can't believe he couldn't get a date for the prom. If I was a girl, I would have gone to the prom with him. Does that sound gay, straight or bi?" Then he killed his father and wounded two students in a home-and-school shooting on August 30, 2006, in Hillsborough, North Carolina.

On the morning of his attack, Castillo sent an email to Columbine High: "Dear Principal, In a few hours you will probably hear about a school shooting in North Carolina. I am responsible for it. I remember Columbine. It is time the world remembered it." He called his plan "Operation Columbine" and, like a number of mass shooters, wore a shirt inscribed "Natural Selection" in honor of Harris. He borrowed another Harris brainchild by nicknaming his shotgun "Arlene," which the Columbiner took from a favorite character in the Doom series of sci-fi novels. Although he planned suicide, Castillo survived and was sentenced to life in prison without hope of parole.

- The Columbine killers are mentioned several times in the written leavings of Kimveer Gill, a paranoid, suicidal, conspiracy-minded Canadian who killed one student and wounded 19 others on September 13, 2006, at Dawson College in Montreal. He referred to Harris and Klebold as "Modern Day Saints," and imitated their fascination with Nazis (writing "Heil Heil Heil" repeatedly in online posts). He also borrowed several of Harris's favored phrases, including "I am God."

- In October 2006, just a few weeks after the Montreal attack, Sebastian Bosse wore a Columbine-inspired black trench coat during his assault on a school in Emsdetten, Germany. Bosse shot five people, although all survived. Like the Columbiners, he killed himself. He referred to Harris several times in his journal, including his all-caps declaration that "ERIC HARRIS IS GOD!" He continued, referring to several other mass shooters, including Harris and Klebold, by their nicknames, REB and VoDKa: "It is scary how similar Eric was to me. Sometimes it seems as if I were to live his life again, as if everything would repeat itself. I am not a copy of REB, VoDKa, Steinhäuser, Gill, Kinkel, Weise or anybody else! I am the advancement of REB!

I learned from his mistakes, the bombs. I learned from his entire life."

- Columbine was a longtime fixation for Seung-Hui Cho, 23, whose attack at Virginia Tech University on April 16, 2007, eclipsed the Columbine death toll. (He killed 32 men and women and himself.) In a video recording, Cho identified with the Columbiners, placing himself in the company of "generation after generation [of] we martyrs, like Eric and Dylan." Cho had written about Columbine in school assignments dating to his adolescence, causing a disturbed teacher to report to administrators that Cho had suggested that "he wanted to repeat Columbine." In turn, several mass shooters have paid homage to Cho.

    Vester Flanagan, who shot and killed two television journalists during a live broadcast in 2015 in Virginia, left a note that read: "I was influenced by Seung-Hui Cho. That's my boy right there. He got NEARLY double the amount that Eric Harris and Dylan Klebold got." (In fact, Cho killed more than twice as many.) Like Harris, Cho has attracted international infamy. Wellington de Oliveira, who killed 12 schoolchildren in 2011 in Brazil, referred to Cho as "a brother."

- Pekka-Eric Auvinen, 18, who murdered eight people and wounded a dozen in a November 2007 school

Dubbed the "YouTube killer," Pekka-Eric Auvinen killed eight people and injured 12 others in a school shooting in southern Finland.

shooting in Tuusula, Finland, was an avid scholar of Columbine. He entitled his journal "Natural Selector's Manifesto," in homage to one of Harris's favorite tropes, and during his rampage he wore a T-shirt that read, "Humanity Is Overrated," another Harris-ism. Like Harris, he compared himself to God, ranted about "retards," and was an admirer of Hitler.

- Karl Pierson was just a toddler in 1999 on the date of the Columbine attack, but he boned up on Harris and Klebold while planning an armed assault on his own suburban Denver high school in 2013. (Pierson, who struggled with psychological problems, stood out among young mass killers by acknowledging that he was not necessarily entirely sane. "I am a psychopath with a superiority complex," he wrote in his journal.) He paraphrased Harris's love–hate platitude—"I am filled with hate, I love it"—and, like Harris, referred to his planned attack as NBK, for *Natural Born Killers* (the title of a gory 1994 movie). Like the Columbiners, he went bowling shortly before his spree, on December 13, 2013, at Arapahoe High School in Centennial, Colorado. As with so many planned mass killings, Pierson failed to bring about widespread destruction. He shot and killed a female classmate, tossed a Molotov cocktail that was a dud, then shot himself dead. Pierson wrote that he acted in retribution for the bullying he had suffered in grade school.

- Alex Hribal, 16, injured 20 in a knife attack on April 9, 2014, at his high school in Murrysville, Pennsylvania. "I would be nothing and this whole event would never occur if it weren't for Eric Harris and Dylan Klebold or Columbine High School," he wrote before the attack. "They worked hard to achieve freedom in heaven. I admire them greatly because they saw something wrong in the world and moved away [from] the herd of sheep to do something about it. They also possessed three crucial things a person needs in order to become a god: intelligence, ideology, and malice (or cruelty) . . .

I became a prophet because I spread the word of a god, Eric Harris."

- John LaDue's plan to attack his school in Waseca, Minnesota, was foiled in April 2014 when a woman called the police about his strange behavior. "My number one idol is Eric Harris," LaDue told an investigator. "I think I just see myself in him. Like he would be the kind of guy I'd want to be with, like, if I knew him. I just thought he was cool."

- Five weeks later, Aaron Ybarra, 26, killed one student and injured two others in a June 5, 2014, shooting at Seattle Pacific University in Washington. "Since Virginia Tech and Columbine, I've been thinking about these a lot," Ybarra wrote in his journal. "I used to feel bad for the ones who were killed, but now Eric Harris and Seung-Hui Cho became my idols. And they guided me 'til today." After the shooting, he told police it would not have happened but for "the guidance of Eric Harris and Seung-Hui Cho in my head . . . Especially Eric Harris. He was a, oh man, he was a master of all shooters." Ybarra, subdued by a student, survived, and was sentenced to 112 years in prison.

- Harris also inspired Randy Stair, 24, who shot and killed three coworkers (and himself) in a Tunkhannock,

Pennsylvania, grocery store on June 8, 2017. "I cannot get Columbine off my mind," he wrote in his journal. He too had several T-shirts emblazoned with "Natural Selection," and he declared that the supermarket he shot up "is officially Columbine High School." Like Alvaro Castillo, Stair expressed his love for Harris, including: "Eric Harris, no homo, but I fucking love you, man! Thank you so fucking much for getting me into guns! When I'm dead I wanna shoot with you, dude. Let's make it happen!" Stair also wrote: "I'm a girl who's been trapped in a man's body for two and a half decades, and I need to get the hell out."

He stood beside his idol in this telling entry: "I guarantee a lot of you reading this feel somewhat similar to me. I'm not a psychopath, I'm a trapped soul eager to get out, only I want to have some fun before I go. Eric Harris was NOT a psychopath. He wanted to fit in, make friends, get laid, and have a good time. He was just in the wrong crowd and group of kids. He was an outcast who should've been respected. I'm the same way—only I was shy and less outgoing. I wanted to make friends DESPERATELY but all I ended up seeing was the bad in people."

Did Harris Spearhead a Revolution?

A long list of other mass shooters left a vivid record of their Columbine studies, from videos to web-browsing footprints to

journals to online forums and social media comments. Nathalie
Paton, a university sociologist in Paris, has found patterns in the
videos left by young killers that support the idea of interconnected
contagion. Her sample includes Auvinen, Bosse, Castillo, Cho,
Gill, and Oliveira. They show off their guns in the videos,
pointing them menacingly toward the camera—and at their own
temples. "This type of video shows them as masculine figures,"
Paton wrote, "rejecting any image of themselves as weak or
'sissies,' corresponding to a previously well-established image of
school shooters." She continued:

> *If the convergence of visual productions allows little
> doubt as to mimicry, examination of stated identifications
> support this idea. School shooters explicitly name or
> represent one another. Oliveira refers to Cho as a brother
> in arms; Castillo points out that his cultural tastes are
> like those of "Eric and Dylan"; Auvinen uses images from
> the Columbine shooting surveillance camera and devotes
> several videos to the Columbine killers. This aspect
> underlines the fact that the boys actively take part in
> associating themselves to a group . . .*
>
> *The role of their videos is pivotal: it shows their
> intrinsic individuality, while portraying a violent identity,
> based on a hyper-normative stereotype of masculinity.
> In their minds, they become anti-heroic icons of modern
> times, thus redefining their identity and reversing the
> roles of domination.*

Harris had fewer role models available in 1999, so he groomed Klebold to join his *folie à deux*. Today's mass shooter fanboys have scores of antecedents to study. To be sure, the killing lineage is far from homogenous. While many of the new cases share methods that build upon the old, each mass shooter is evil in his own unique way. At the same time, psychologists and public safety authorities are concerned that today's public has grown inured to incomprehensible violence. They also worry that tomorrow's mass killers are playing a game to outdo yesterday's because it will extend their inglorious moment. So did Harris accomplish his goal of spearheading an insurrection by like-minded young men? The mass killings that followed him suggest that he did, in a sense. Writing in the journal *American Behavioral Scientist*, New York sociologist Ralph W. Larkin argued that he changed the narrative, at the very least:

> *The Columbine rampage has become a cultural script for many subsequent rampage shooters. For some, it was a record to be exceeded; for others, it was an incitement; for others, it was emulated in their own rampages; for still others, it was a tradition to be honored in their own attacks . . . Although they did not kick-start a revolution, Klebold and Harris established a new paradigm by which all subsequent rampage shootings must be measured.*

They reinforced the unfortunate male ethic that equates masculinity with violence, provided a groveling pit for other despairing young men and, most bracingly, set a target to surpass.

Wikipedia and other online venues keep scorecards on mass shootings. You may be surprised to learn that the Columbine massacre, with 13 dead victims, is no longer in the American top ten, having been surpassed by the likes of Las Vegas (58 killed), Orlando (49), Virginia Tech (32), Sandy Hook (27), the Sutherland Springs, Texas, church (26), and the Parkland, Florida, high school (17). Each of the top five in terms of casualties has occurred since 2007. Many advocates argue that the media and authorities ought to de-emphasize body counts and discourage graphics with national rankings, since they inevitably serve as a goal for the homicidally inclined. That seems like a serpentine route to address the Columbine disease. Those most engaged by the subject matter will find the data. For example, when news spread in 2011 that Anders Breivik had killed 77 people in Norway, Sandy Hook killer Adam Lanza posted a note online that someone had "finally" bested the record of Woo Bum-kon, a sick and suicidal South Korean cop who killed 56 people there in 1982. These people know the score—and who's winning.

Chapter 2.
"You'll All Know Who I Am"

A few weeks before he shot up an Oregon college campus in 2015, Christopher Harper-Mercer's ears pricked up over the recognition that one of his "godly" idols had attained. Vester Flanagan had won acute notoriety by adding an attention-grabbing twist to murder: On August 26, 2015, the former television reporter—fired for belligerence in 2013—exacted revenge against his former employer by shooting a reporter, a photographer, and a news source during a live remote interview for a CBS affiliate in Roanoke, Virginia. The two journalists were killed, though the source survived, and Flanagan shot himself to death five hours later. Although the death toll was meager, the live-TV angle brought an avalanche of attention to the formerly obscure man. This resonated with Harper-Mercer:

> *On an interesting note, I have noticed that so many people*
> *like him are all alone and unknown, yet when they spill a*

little blood, the whole world knows who they are. A man who was known by no one is now known by everyone. His face splashed across every screen, his name across the lips of every person on the planet, all in the course of one day. Seems the more people you kill, the more you're in the limelight.

Gory Pathway to Fame

Peter Langman, the school shooting expert, broke it down: "For those who feel like they are nobody, the path to becoming somebody is very simple—get a gun and shoot a lot of people." Valery Fabrikant, a disgruntled faculty member who killed four colleagues at Montreal's Concordia University in 1992, used nearly identical language in describing what he called the "North American way" of settling disputes. "I know how people get what they want," Fabrikant wrote. "They shoot a lot of people." Nikolas Cruz followed that formula when he attacked his former high school in Parkland, Florida, on Valentine's Day in 2018, killing 14 students and three staff members. He introduced himself to the world in a series of three brief cellphone videos.

"I am going to be the next school shooter of 2018," he said. "When you see me on the news, you'll all know who I am. You're all going to die . . . All the kids in school will run in fear and hide. From the wrath of my power, they will know who I am."

And before he shot up a political event in Arizona in 2011, killing six, the mentally troubled Jared Loughner was cognizant

of his impending infamy. He wrote online: "WOW! I'm glad i
didn't kill myself. I'll see you on National T.V.!"

Adam Lankford, a University of Alabama criminologist,
told a gathering of journalists in 2018 that mass shooters are
all too aware of the phenomenon by now. "When someone is
desperate for fame or attention," Lankford said, "committing
a high-profile mass killing is one of the only guaranteed ways
to get it. In many cases, winning a Super Bowl or Academy
Award garners less media attention than committing one of
these crimes."

As the French philosopher Jean Rostand famously put it:
"Kill one man and you are a murderer. Kill a million and you are
a conqueror. Kill them all and you are a god." The manifestos and
more meager musings of many mass shooters frequently refer
to godly power, and across many cultures over many centuries
the taking of a human life has been regarded as a superhuman
act. Like Florida's Cruz, many mass killers have cited the sense
of power it brings—or their hope that it will. The higher the
body count, the greater the presumed eminence. Harper-Mercer
paid homage to high-count killers as "people who stand with the
gods," including "The Columbine kids," Connecticut school
shooter Adam Lanza, and Seung-Hui Cho, the Virginia Tech
shooter. And Lanza understood the potential for glorification,
writing: "Just look at how many fans you can find for all different
types of mass murderers, and beyond these fans are countless
more people who can sympathize with them."

Self-glorification has become a troubling motivation in
an increasing number of large-scale shootings in the U.S. and

Europe. Ian Buruma wrote in *The Guardian* about Norway's Anders Breivik:

> *What such killers crave more than anything else is maximum publicity, fame, attention. The sad irony is that politicians, journalists, bloggers, and a million commentators, including myself, invariably do everything to grant them their wish. Worldwide publicity transforms these misfits into heroic or villainous representatives of global religions, political ideologies and even entire civilizations.*

Early Spotlight Seekers

It is not a new mania. Many serial killers, basking in criminal star power, have teased the media or the police with correspondence: London's Jack the Ripper, northern California's Zodiac Killer, New York City's Son of Sam, and the BTK Strangler of Wichita, Kansas, to name just a few from a very long list. A certain type of criminal id has always yearned for the spotlight, from lowly pickpockets and sneak thieves to Mafia *capo dei capi* like the New York mobster John Gotti—and his wife. Long before her family became reality TV stars, Victoria Gotti once sent me an enraged letter urging me to "walk a mile in my moccasins" after I wrote a column describing how her son, Junior, had threatened to chop off my head. She didn't mind a bit when her missive became front-page news.

Fame was also on the mind of Charles Whitman as he ascended a tower on the Austin campus of the University of Texas in 1966. Whitman, a suicidal, psychologically fragile man who was distressed by family and career problems, killed 15 people and wounded 31, picking them off like ants on the ground from his lofty redoubt. The case is regarded by some as the earliest modern American mass shooting—although choosing a "first" is subjective since the U.S. has a long, bloody record of mass-casualty atrocities dating back more than a century. Whitman's biographer, Gary Lavergne, wrote that the killer was aware of the Klieg lights that had been trained on two rather ordinary murderers by Truman Capote's *In Cold Blood*, published in January 1966. Seven months later, on August 1, Whitman sought the same sort of lasting true crime infamy. "He climbed the Tower because he wanted to die in a big way," Lavergne wrote. He succeeded. Five decades later, his name is still synonymous with U.S. mass killings.

Circle of Death

Whitman's homicides were followed closely by a fame-seeking copycat teenager named Robert Smith, who attacked women at a beauty school in Mesa, Arizona. He forced his victims to lie on the floor—in a "circle of death," the press called it—then executed five of them with pistol shots to the back of the head. When a cop asked him why he did it, Smith replied: "I wanted to kill about 40 people so I could make a name for myself. I wanted people to know who I was." The story was front-page news: "Boy Kills Five to Make Himself Well Known." But as Napoleon is said to have quipped: "Glory is fleeting, but obscurity is forever."

Smith did not achieve the transcendent infamy of other mass shooters, including his inspiration, Whitman. Outside of Mesa, only dedicated crime aficionados and the loved ones of his victims will recall his name today. And his obscurity drags on. Smith has been locked up since the day of the shooting, passing more than 50 birthdays behind bars in Arizona. His most recent prison mugshot shows a gray-haired man with a combover staring wide-eyed into the camera lens with a look of weary resignation. Freedom is not forthcoming. He has been denied parole repeatedly, most recently in March 2018.

I Don't Like Mondays

That an 18-year-old like Smith would kill for notoriety no longer seems shocking. We've grown accustomed to this particular sickness, including a rare example of a female mass shooter. On Monday January 29, 1979, 16-year-old Brenda Spencer used a .22-caliber rifle to ping 30 shots at children queued up outside an elementary school in San Diego, California, injuring eight kids and killing the principal and a janitor. Asked about her motive, she famously explained: "I just don't like Mondays. I did this because it's a way to cheer up the day. Nobody likes Mondays." While holed up in her house later, she grew giddy to learn there were TV cameras outside. "That's great!" she exclaimed.

Just before her attack, Spencer told a friend: "Wait until Monday, and see what I'm going to do. It might even be big enough to make the news." She made the news all right, and her murders were the subject of a 1979 hit song by Bob Geldof's Irish band, the Boomtown Rats. But like Arizona's Smith she

In 1979, 16-year-old Brenda Spencer shot up an elementary school in San Diego because she didn't "like Mondays. Nobody likes Mondays."

did not ascend to the top tier of the American pantheon of mass killers. And in common with Smith, Spencer has endured a long, obscure existence for four decades in the California penal system. She has been denied parole nine times since 1993.

Lust for Media Attention

Since Spencer's moment in the media sun, many headline-grabbing killers have predicted their own notoriety. Before he shot and killed a teacher at his Lake Worth, Florida, school in 2000, Nathaniel Brazill, 13, told a classmate, "Watch, I'm going to be all over the news," and another fame-seeker, Sebastian Bosse, 18, the 2006 German school shooter, bragged to friends: "I'm going to be really big one day . . . Everybody will talk about me." Robert Hawkins, who at age 19 killed eight people and himself in a 2007 shopping mall shooting in Omaha, Nebraska, suggested in a suicide note that media attention was a silver lining of his murders.

> I know everyone will remember me as some sort of monster, but please understand that I just don't want to be a burden on the ones that I care for my entire life. I just want to take a few pieces of shit with me.

He expressed regrets toward his parents and friends but added: "Just think tho, I'm gonna be fuckin' famous."

Jack Sawyer, a Vermont teenager whose school shooting plans were foiled in 2018 when a friend tipped off the police, kept a journal in which he all but salivated at his expected future glory.

"I will be immortal from my actions," Sawyer wrote. "The mass chaos I'll create will leave everyone hopeless and distraught and fearful of their every next step." In another case, lust for attention alerted the authorities—and perhaps averted a shooting—when school officials in Mishawaka, Indiana, found a notebook in a 16-year-old boy's locker. The teenager had written: "I wanna break the current shooting record. I wanna get instant recognition."

And during a three-hour standoff following his 2016 assault on an Orlando, Florida, nightclub, Omar Mateen repeatedly checked Facebook, to see whether news of his attack had gone viral on social media. After barricading himself in the building where nearly 50 men and women lay dead or dying from his hand, he called a television station and gleefully introduced himself by saying: "It's me. I'm the shooter." Jared Loughner, who wounded U.S. Representative Gabrielle Giffords and killed six others in 2011 in Tucson, Arizona, crowed: "I'll see you on national TV!"

The potential for infamy was central to the planning that Jesse Osborne, a 14-year-old South Carolina boy, put into the 2016 attack that left his father and an unrelated child dead. As usual in these cases, he was shooting for many more victims. "I think I'll probably most likely kill around 50 or 60," he wrote in his journal. "If I get lucky, maybe 150." He googled terms such as "top 10 mass shooters," "youngest mass murderer," and "10 youngest murderers in history." "I HAVE TO BEAT ADAM LAZA . . . at least 40," Osborne wrote nine days before his attack, misspelling the surname of Lanza, the Sandy Hook killer who took 27 lives.

Omar Mateen's ex-wife said he was "mentally unstable and mentally ill,"
yet he had a license to work as a security guard and for "concealed [gun]
carry" in Florida. He also had a history of steroid abuse.

Columbiners' Movie Hopes

As they planned their 1999 Colorado high school attack, Eric Harris and Dylan Klebold understood that the record they left of their lives and motivations would give them prominence in popular culture. On their "basement tape" videos, they mused over how their story would be told on film. Harris said he favored "a lot of foreshadowing and dramatic irony," and Klebold avidly replied:

> *Directors will be fighting over this story. I know we're gonna have followers because we're so fucking god-like. We're not exactly human—we have human bodies but we've evolved into one step above you, fucking human shit. We actually have fucking self-awareness.*

They agreed that either Steven Spielberg or Quentin Tarantino would be a good fit as a director. In his journal, Harris mused: "I wonder if anyone will write a book on me. Sure is a ton of symbolism, double meanings, themes, appearance vs. reality shit going on here. Oh well, it better be fuckin' good if it is written." He needn't have wondered. He plays a lead role in more than a dozen books and features in countless other books, scholarly reports, and films. A Google search of his name returns about 150 million results, so he got the infamy he craved.

The lust for media attention among large-scale killers has been a clear continuum since Columbine, with murderers in competition with one another, using body counts as a scorecard. Adam Lankford, the Alabama criminologist whose research explores the intersection of fame and criminality, believes that Harris and Klebold created a mass murder "tipping point." He told me:

> There is no doubt that human beings have sought recognition for millennia and that at least some criminals have done so long before the modern problem of mass shootings . . . I think Columbine is the most influential case because of the amount of media attention it received and the number of copycats it inspired and continues to inspire. But of course Columbine's impact is exacerbated by the social context: in our culture, fame-seeking is on the rise, narcissistic tendencies are on the rise, the distinction between fame/infamy is increasingly blurred . . . If Columbine had happened in the 1960s, I don't think it has the same effect even if it received the same amount of media attention, because fewer people were desperate for fame at any cost. The problem is the media is rewarding and incentivizing mass shootings at precisely the same time when people are more desperate for these rewards and more responsive to these incentives than ever before.

Fame-Seekers Are Mostly Young

Lankford's research suggests that younger people are more likely to seek notoriety through violence. His 2016 study of rampage shooters concluded that those seeking fame averaged about 20 years old while those with other motivations were nearly 15 years older on average. He said young people today "put a much higher priority on being famous than their older counterparts."

In a 2018 journal article with colleague Eric Madfis, Lankford concluded that the media freely bestow precious publicity on young mass killers. They wrote:

> . . . During their attack months, some mass killers received more highly valued coverage than some of the most famous American celebrities, including Kim Kardashian, Brad Pitt, Tom Cruise, Johnny Depp, and Jennifer Aniston . . . Most mass killers received more coverage from newspapers and broadcast/cable news than the public interest they generated through online searches and Twitter seems to warrant. Unfortunately, this media attention constitutes free advertising for mass killers that may increase the likelihood of copycats.

Count Randy Stair in that club. At age 24, he was fed up with life and obsessed with criminal fame as he prepared in 2017 to shoot up the grocery store where he worked near Scranton, Pennsylvania. For seven months before, he compiled videos, his self-described "Suicide Tapes," and a handwritten, 237-page journal filled with familiar nihilistic rants like this:

> What makes someone as innocent-looking as me want to cause mass devastation and manipulation? . . . I've hated humans my entire life. I hated making friends, "socializing" amongst my classmates, and just overall

being spoken to. Humans are <u>WORTHLESS</u>. We are living, breathing, moving trash. I don't care what you say; life is a never-ending simulation of hell.

Just before he began his rampage one June night, Stair took time to post links to his journal materials on his Twitter account. Desperate to ensure wide distribution, he included information on where to find backups in case they were taken down by the authorities. Among many other things, he ruminated in his journal about his need for attention but, interestingly, he also mulled over whether he deserved a national spotlight: He knew his body count would be modest because he planned a midnight attack, when the store would be empty of customers:

> *It's crazy to think if I go through with the plan to kill my coworkers I'll make the news headlines . . . Sometimes you gotta do evil deeds to be famous; it's fate, nothing more, nothing less. Granted, shooting 2-3 coworkers in a store and taking your own life isn't national news-worthy, [but] it gets your name out there. As I said, I'd shoot up the store in the day but I'd be neutralized and stopped fast. Someone would definitely have a gun in their purse. I'll take the "sure thing" and do what I know will work. I want to leave my mark, even if only one guy is killed . . .*

A month before the shooting took place, Stair had convinced himself that he was bound for glory.

*I'll be filled with power beyond imaginable after those
first few shots are fired . . . I'll be the talk of Luzerne
County and then a story nationwide. Screw fame, gimme
infamy! . . . In 25 days I'll go into the history books. The
human race will remember my name for a century . . .
I can't wait to inhale the delicious scent of shock from
everyone who knows me.*

I doubt he will go down in history because, as he predicted, he
has too much competition in the crime atrocity niche. But these
riffs on infamy and obscurity crop up frequently in the written
leavings of many others, including the three-page suicide note
of Geddy Kramer, 19, a security guard who shot up a FedEx
warehouse in Kennesaw, Georgia, in 2014. He wounded six
people, then shot himself in the head—the only fatality. Here
is the concluding paragraph of his farewell, a mashup of many
manifesto themes, including sexual frustrations:

*This is my own doing. I'm a sociopath. I want to hurt
people. Maybe a part of this is also the fact that a life
lived in infamy is better than just another nobody . . . If
my self-esteem was at a point other than negative and I
grew a pair to actually get myself laid, maybe I'd be alive
now. I'm in my happy place. I'm in my happy place. I'm
in my happy place.*

He seemed to be trying to convince himself with that final
tombstone platitude. But infamy's upside occurred early to Elliot

Rodger, California's "kissless virgin," who targeted women in his 2014 shooting rampage. In his long autobiographical account of his life, Rodger recalled this epiphany from his adolescence:

> As middle school approached its ultimate end, I was having a miserable time there. I was extremely unpopular, widely disliked, and viewed as the weirdest kid in the school. I had to act weird in order to gain attention . . . Infamy is better than total obscurity . . . It felt horrible to be teased and bullied . . . It caused me a lot of pain and anger . . . but at the same time I got a kick out of getting so much attention . . . I never knew how to gain positive attention, only negative.

Ancient Attention-Seeker

Negative attention is not a contemporary concept. History is rife with horrendous criminal acts committed with the goal of self-glorification. Perhaps most infamously, in the fourth century BC an obscure Greek named Herostratus hoped to go down in history when he set fire to the Temple of Artemis, one of the wonders of the ancient world. Twice the size of the Parthenon, with dozens of gleaming, 40-foot marble pillars, the 200-year-old temple at Ephesus was built as a monument to a revered Greek goddess, and it was a magnet for pilgrims.

Nevertheless, Herostratus was delighted to bring it down with fire in 356 BC, and made no attempt to hide his crime. To the contrary, he declared himself the arsonist and admitted his motive: To go down in history. He paid a dear price, though, including torture and execution. But the Ephesian authorities added a deeper layer of punishment by subjecting him to *damnatio memoriae*, or condemnation of memory. In other words, he was sentenced to obscurity, where no one was allowed to speak his name. The fact that it survives today, however, is proof that the punishment failed. Ancient scriveners kept the details alive, and references to the condemned Greek turn up in classical literature—Chaucer, Cervantes, Melville, and others. Shakespeare nicely summarized the absurdity of the sentence in *Richard III*:

> *Th' aspiring youth that fir'd th' Ephesian Dome*
> *Out-lives in Fame the pious Fool that rais'd it . . .*

The Bard added that fame from "evil deeds" outlasts that of benevolence.

She was speaking of terrorism, not temple arsons, but Margaret Thatcher, the former British prime minister, captured the essence of this notoriety conundrum when she pointed out that the "oxygen of publicity" is needed to sustain such criminals. In a 2005 book, crime historian Albert Borowitz defined the "Herostratus Syndrome": "The criminal feels an enhancement of power in the form of self-glorification (the achievement of name recognition) or self-aggrandizement (the demonstration of capacity for destruction through the accomplishment of a flaunting act that will live in infamy)."

Media Sensationalism

Ralph W. Larkin, the New York sociologist, has argued that the Columbiners—enabled by the media—remade school shootings, traditionally regarded as acts of revenge, into political statements. He wrote:

> *Klebold and Harris were overtly political in their motivations to destroy their school . . . One of the cultural scripts that is a consequence of the Columbine shootings is that the shooters engage in their rampages to "make a statement." The body count, almost always innocent bystanders, exists primarily as a method of generating media attention . . . Tragedy has been converted to sensation and sensation is operationalized into viewership, Nielsen points, and market share, which is then materialized in advertising revenues. The communities in which rampage shootings occur are victimized twice: first by the shootings themselves and second by the media who rampage through their communities to get the story.*

That stings a bit to this longtime crime journalist, who has covered more murders—mass and more discreet—than he cares to recall. On the other hand, the press as a target is about as easy to hit as those pitiable unarmed Columbine students. But I must admit that I made the same arguments in my 1996 book, *Scooped*, a self-examination of media sensationalism after I had trudged away from my job as chief crime reporter for the tabloid *New*

York Daily News. As part of my research for that book, I asked a professional peer, a Cleveland newspaper courts reporter, why we seemed to use so much precious news space on sensational but aberrational crime stories. He replied: "Because people like to read them." He did not add "Duh," though he could have.

News pandering was a professional focus for the late Bonnie Bucqueroux, a longtime Michigan State University professor with a special interest in how the media treat crime victims.

She once said:

> *The truth is that evil is a compelling thing to look at. The question is, how much do we pander to our curiosity, and to what extent do we want to show our children that this is a viable way for a person to garner attention, because we know from our kids that those who can't get attention through positive behavior will turn to negative behavior to get attention?*

That includes not just kids, but killer kids like Harris and Klebold, et al. So how should journalists report mass shootings when they risk playing into a young man's orgasmic anticipation of public glorification? That quandary harks back to questions as old as crime reporting itself, which was institutionalized 200 years ago in the Western press.

Beginnings of Crime Reporting

In their earliest iterations, newspapers were filled with monotonous records of commerce—the comings and goings of ships, for example—interspersed with political diatribes. Then in 1821 the *London Morning Herald* tried to liven up the ink by sending scribe John Wight to attend night sessions of the Bow Street Court, from which he gave readers a kaleidoscopic view of the city's colorful underclass of drunks, sex workers, and grifters. The subject matter proved shocking—and irresistible—to readers. Police and court reporting, along with the attendant criticism by high-collared snobs, soon made its way across the Atlantic. Criticism came from many quarters, including newspapers themselves. This is from an 1828 editorial in the *New York Statesman*:

> *We deem it of little benefit to the cause of morals thus to familiarize the community, and especially the younger parts of it, to the details of misdemeanors and crimes. It is a contemplation that, without any possible good, at once exposes the heart to taint and the mind to perversion. Besides, it suggests to the novice in vice all the means of becoming expert in its devices. The dexterity of one knave, arrested and sent to State Prison, is adopted from newspaper instruction by others yet at large . . . And then we ask whether it is congenial to pure feeling and sentiment, either to register these matters on the one hand, or to delight in their perusal on the other? We think not.*

Another critic, a patrician New Yorker named Philip Hone, presaged the glorification of mass shooters when he suggested that the gullible "are prone to look with some degree of admiration upon those of a more daring and atrocious character, and their admiration leads them insensibly to sympathize with the perpetrators." James Gordon Bennett, whose *New York Herald* embraced crime reporting in the 1830s, had this reply: "An exact and correct record or crime—ingenious crime, not vulgar drunken brawls—is useful as a warning and a beacon for others to avoid."

Shooters' Lists of Interests

I can't say that most of the news content about mass killers could be called a useful beacon. By and large, journalists seek answers to the same fundamental questions we have asked for generations: who, what, when, where, why, and how? To be sure, we've wandered down some trippy alleys in our pursuits. For example, the media's track record over the past two decades of obsessing on a mass killer's music, movie, and video game preferences—as though they offered clues to his particular psychopathy—has now prompted spotlighted felons to post this information for our benefit. It has gotten absurd. This is from Chris Harper-Mercer's journal, which he organized in the familiar Wikipedia form of subcategories:

> *Now for the part I'm sure the media will love. My interests. My interests include listening to music, watching movies, Internet piracy. My only solace in online life is posting on Kat.cr as the user lithium_love. I mostly have uploaded porno, ebooks, things like that. That has been my only joy*

*in life. I will leave a sign on my profile there for any who
wish to see it.*

He listed 11 bands and five movies. ("Check out what I've
uploaded. You may find our tastes are more similar than you
realize.") He then added these essentials:

Favorite colors are Red and Black
Favorite food is potatoes
Favorite drink is soymilk

There are other examples, from marquee mass shooters to those
who escaped notice. Some link this strange trend to Columbine's
Harris, who dropped many references to popular culture in
the record he left behind, but it predates Harris. In 1991, for
example, Gang Lu, a suicidal Chinese student who killed three
professors and a classmate at the University of Iowa, dedicated
the third paragraph of his suicide note to American film history:

*My first movie seen in the US is "About Last Night" the
evening I passed my comprehensive exams. My favorite
movies include "No Way Out," "Die Hard," "Indiana Jones,"
and Clint Eastwood's movies where a single cowboy
fights against a group of incorporated bad guys who pick
on little guys at their will or cover up each other's ass.*

Jon Romano, a depressed teenager, left a 450-word explanation
hours before he shot up his high school near Albany, New York,

in 2004. Half of the note consisted of a list of his favorite things, including TV shows, music ("Country music! Toby Keith"), and films. He added: "I like to laugh! Comedies are good! I'm not what the media says I should be." (His shots injured one person; he has been locked up for 14 years as of 2018.) Geddy Kramer, the suicidal Georgia FedEx warehouse shooter from 2014, included a one-page addendum to his brief suicide note that he labeled "Some favorites." Here is what he wanted the world to know:

Bands:	*Rammstein*
	KMFDM
	Slipknot
Entertainers:	*George Carlin*
	Bill Maher
	Lewis Black
	Bill Burr
Hobbies:	*Video Games*
	Jacking off

Several mass killers have included FAQs—frequently asked questions—in their manifestos or journals. Harper-Mercer's FAQ section was mercifully brief. ("Q. How come you've not had a girlfriend, are you gay? A. No I'm not gay, girls just didn't want me. As I said before they went for the thug blacks. Q. Are you mentally ill? A. No I'm not. Just because I'm in communion with the Dark Forces doesn't mean I'm crazy.")

Norway's Breivik included a FAQ component in his vast manifesto that tried—but failed—to rationalize his racist

Islamophobia. I won't stupefy you with his answers, but here is a sample of his questions: "a. What about the Crusades? b. If Islam is violent, why are so many Muslims peaceful? c. What about the violent passages in the Bible? . . ." Similarly, Breivik included a Q&A with himself that slogs on for more than 65 single-spaced pages. That's barely a blip in his *Compendium* manifesto, which runs to just shy of a million words—five times the length of *Mein Kampf*.

To wade through Breivik's work in total, the average reader would have to surrender two full weeks of reading—eight hours a day for at least ten days. And what might you learn from the time spent? Yes, he includes a favorites list, which goes on for dozens of pages. Here is his index: "Q: Name your favourite: a. music, b. destination, c. possession or item with high affection value, d. clothing brand, e. eau de toilette, f. ball sport, g. football team, h. comedian, i. food, j. movie, k. type of architecture and interior design direction, l. beer, m. drink, n. books."

I will spare you the answers.

Do we really need to know that the favorite colors of an alienated Oregon school shooter are red and black? That an un-hinged Norwegian racist prefers Egoiste cologne? That a hope-lessly horny California man-child wasted his life playing World of Warcraft? It seems like too much information, though I will admit that in years past I was among the journalists sweeping up this sort of seemingly irrelevant miscellany while scrambling against the deadline clock (and competitors) to create a portrait of the latest newly minted mass killer or other form of crime celebrity.

Before the Internet age, journalists gathered those details by climbing apartment house steps and knocking on doors—

or at least working the phones. Killers bent on infamy today do this legwork for us by, in effect, crafting the first draft of their personal narrative, often by casting themselves as heroic victims, not cowards who target the innocent. That is a failing of contemporary journalism. If only for a few news cycles, this rush to the Internet for manifestos or social media notes—which journalists distill into the ubiquitous "portrait-of-a-gunman" stories—makes us cogs in the self-glorification they seek.

Minimizing the Details

I'm not convinced that we've reached a full-scale backlash against media mindlessness, but changes seem afoot. Many newspapers and broadcast outlets now minimize the use of the names and photographs of mass killers, particularly after the initial story cycles. Former FBI Director James Comey, speaking at a 2016 press briefing on the Orlando nightclub shooting, gave this explanation of why it makes sense to obscure these identities:

> *You will notice that I'm not using the killer's name . . .*
> *Part of what motivates sick people to do this kind of*
> *thing is some twisted notion of fame or glory. And I don't*
> *want to be part of that for the sake of the victims and*
> *their families—and so that other twisted minds don't*
> *think that this is a path to fame and recognition.*

The February 2018 school shooting in Parkland, Florida, may prove to be a tipping point. Social media-savvy students there at Marjory Stoneman Douglas High School have forced several dialogues—about the American political morass on mass shootings, gun control, and the media's willingness to give airtime and ink to attention-craving criminals. Students and parents from the school were acutely critical when the media aired the shooter's video boasts, including: "You'll all know who I am."

"This is what he wants," tweeted Aalayah Eastmond, a student survivor who was inspired into activism. "Don't let him trend." Her classmate Alex Wind got 37,000 likes and more than 8,000 retweets of this message:

> He deserves no attention. Here's who does: Alyssa Alhadeff, Scott Beigel, Martin Duque, Nicholas Dworet, Aaron Feis, Jaime Guttenberg, Chris Hixon, Luke Hoyer, Cara Loughran, Gina Montalto, Joaquin Oliver, Alaina Petty, Meadow Pollack, Helena Ramsay, Alex Schachter, Carmen Schentrup, Peter Wang.

Those were the killer's victims. "I think our society needs to make him like a black box with a white X," Lori Alhadeff—whose daughter, Alyssa, was killed at the school—told *The New York Times*. "We need to stop giving him a face, because this evil will just continue to happen if our society keeps glorifying school shooters."

The National Rifle Association clings like crows to roadkill to the questionable notion that video games and music videos inspire mass killers. But it also finds itself in strange fellowship with the Parkland activists when it comes to mass media criticism.

This is what longtime NRA CEO Wayne LaPierre had to say after the Sandy Hook School shooting in 2012:

> *The truth is that our society is populated by an unknown number of genuine monsters . . . They walk among us every single day, and does anybody really believe that the next Adam Lanza isn't planning his attack on a school he's already identified at this very moment? How many more copycats are waiting in the wings for their moment of fame from a national media machine that rewards them with wall-to-wall attention and a sense of identity that they crave, while provoking others to try to make their mark?*

"No Notoriety" Media Campaign

And yet "Who" is the first of the by-rote questions that would-be reporters are taught to ask in their very first journalism class, and we will never stop seeking that answer. But can we be smarter to mitigate glorification? Lankford, the Alabama criminologist, and his research partner Eric Madfis, have suggested four common-sense guidelines based on protocols that many media outlets are experimenting with:

1. *Don't name the perpetrator.*
2. *Don't use photos or likenesses of the perpetrator.*
3. *Stop using the names, photos, or likenesses of past perpetrators.*

4. *Report everything else about these crimes in as much detail as desired.*

Their idea, endorsed by more than 140 other academicians, builds on "No Notoriety," a media campaign initiated by Tom and Caren Teves, whose son, Alex, was one of the 12 people killed in a July 2012 movie theater shooting in Aurora, Colorado. The campaign's message is simple: "No name, no photo, no notoriety." It can be done. In May 2018, the *Times* published a long story that explored mass shooting contagion, in which it cited a half-dozen shootings by admirers of the Columbiners but did not identify any of them. The story noted:

> *There have been growing calls for withholding the names and biographies of school gunmen from newspaper and television coverage. The New York Times regularly identifies and profiles the perpetrators, though in order to focus attention on the issue of school shootings and not on the gunmen themselves, this article does not name any of them.*

Likewise, some broadcasters say they are trying to minimize the attention on shooters, focusing instead on victims. Will that strategy stop the American epidemic of mass shootings? Almost certainly not, considering the liberal availability of weapons of war. But it might help deflect attention from the killers who crave it, and that seems like a modest step in the direction of moral obligation.

Like many others, Lankford has suggested that a chain of fame-seeking rampage shooters with leap-frogging body counts surely lies ahead as long as these would-be killers know that their identities will be etched in crime infamy. He wrote in a journal article that mass killers are now "directly competing with each other for fame" and "choosing targets or attack methods that will make them seem new, different, or innovative." I asked Lankford what sort of reactions his suggestions to dim or darken the marquee lights for criminals have drawn from the media. He replied:

> *I've communicated with many media members, journalists, etc. on this subject, and their responses have varied. Most are interested in the research, agree about the consequences of media coverage of mass shooters, and wish that media coverage could change in helpful ways while allowing them to continue to do their job and report the news. There are differing views about what types of changes would be best (ideally) and what would actually be feasible. Many say something like, "You're probably right, but I don't think the media will ever change," but I think their cynicism is misplaced.*
>
> *But some have been in complete denial. I spoke with the editor in charge of a major media organization, and it was like talking to the head of the NRA about the consequences of guns. Honestly, it was shameful, and I wish our conversation would have been public so people would see for themselves. More broadly, however, I do think the media are slowly becoming more aware of their*

role in this problem and gradually adjusting the nature of their coverage. After the killing at the Capital Gazette *newspaper* [in June 2018 in Annapolis, Maryland], *for example, the coverage of the perpetrator that I saw was more restrained (and hopefully not just because media members were the victims).*

Chapter 3.
How Killers Are Made

"What is this—a country or a slaughterhouse?" Andrew Tully, a nationally syndicated American newspaper columnist, was compelled to ask that question in 1982 after a Pennsylvania spree murder that seemed to be the nadir of U.S. crime atrocities. "Mass murder has become part of the American way of life," Tully declared. "It is a style, a vogue, we are forced to live with every day." Readers surely felt the shuddering in his words. The crime that moved Tully was "unthinkable," to use the adjective that must now be considered archaic.

Mothers and Children Slaughtered

On September 25, 1982, George Banks, a 40-year-old Pennsylvanian with a teetering grip on reality, went on a murderous jag against his own flesh and blood. His 13 victims included five of his children and four different women who had given birth to them. The case was an aberration in that Banks was black—or, more precisely, the son of mixed-race parents, a white mother and a black father—whereas most mass killings in the

U.S. (and Europe) are committed by white men. At the same time, Banks was a template as an early adapter of the semi-automatic assault rifle—the Colt AR-15 in his case—as the preferred mass murder weapon.

Mental Issues

His clear mental issues also made him part of another pattern that has since come into sharp relief. Some experts argue that mental illness among mass shooters is overstated because the diagnoses came retrospectively, after the violent incident, but by most counts at least half of mass murderers exhibit serious symptoms of one form of psychopathy or another. And some argue persuasively that the crimes themselves are prima facie evidence of mental illness.

Pennsylvania's George Banks had worked for a couple of years as a prison guard at Camp Hill, near the state capital of Harrisburg. He raised red flags in the summer of 1982 when he warned his penitentiary colleagues about a looming "race war," and among other examples of disturbing behavior he claimed to guards and prisoners alike that Camp Hill prison grub was poisoned. As a result, he was suspended during the first week of September and barred from returning without a thorough psychiatric examination. His criminal defense attorney later pegged Banks's mental problems to racial issues. He had struggled with racial identity throughout his life and felt alienated from both his parents' races.

"I got the impression he felt he was being rejected by blacks and whites, and he took pressure from both sides," a black friend told a reporter.

Banks had romantic relationships with both black and white women, including a seven-year marriage to Doris Banks, who was black. At the time of his breakdown, Banks was living communally with three women and four of his children in a rambling house on rugged Schoolhouse Lane in Wilkes-Barre, Pennsylvania, 125 miles (200 km) northwest of New York City. At the same time, he was engaged in an acrimonious custody battle involving a son he had fathered with another woman, Sharon Mazzillo.

Killing Spree

After a gin-sotted Friday night, Banks awoke early Saturday and donned military fatigues and a T-shirt inscribed, "Kill 'em all . . . Let God sort it out!" He marched from room to room with his assault rifle, murdering three women and five children, ages eleven, six, four, two and one. (The four youngest were his offspring.) After that, he left the house and shot two neighbors, killing one of them, and then drove five miles to Mazzillo's trailer park home, where he ended his spree by killing the woman, their five-year-old son, and her mother and nephew. Banks holed up in a vacant house, where he kept police at bay for four hours, at one point declaring: "Today is a good day to die."

Ultimately he surrendered and confessed, saying he wanted to spare his mixed-race children the same torments he had suffered. His attorney argued for an insanity verdict at his trial, but jurors were not swayed. They convicted him of the 13 murders and recommended the death penalty. Thirty-five years later, in 2018, Banks was still alive, at age 76, after courts ruled on three different occasions that he was mentally incompetent to face execution. One shrink described Banks as "psychotic, delusional, and irrational."

Here's something else that seems irrational: Unless you were cognizant and alive in northeastern Pennsylvania in 1982, you probably have no recollection of this abominable murder case that stirred the country back then, prompting a prominent columnist to ponder how and why the American soul had been lost. I am intimately familiar with this American mass-murder amnesia. Every other Sunday since 1999 I have written about archival murder cases in "The Justice Story," a true crime feature published in the *New York Daily News* for nearly a century. In researching and writing 500 of these columns, I've unearthed scores of forgotten atrocities that were treated as seminal events in their day—until fresh savagery shunted them aside.

Defining Mass Murder

Mass murder is an inconstant term but it is generally defined as a cluster of killings committed in close geographic proximity over a brief period. (Serial killings, by contrast, are homicides committed by the same person over an extended period—weeks, months, or even years.) After years of disagreement among researchers about the definition of "mass," the FBI and most others now say any body count of four or greater qualifies as a mass murder. The term has appeared in the press for more than a century, including in a *New York Sun* story in 1900 about a rampage killing by a passenger on a Swedish steamship that left the captain and four others dead. It was used sporadically from the 1930s onward to describe both war crimes and familicides, the murder–suicides that were a predominant form of large-scale homicide last century.

James Alan Fox and Jack Levin, long-tenured crime sociologists at Northeastern University in Boston, helped bring the phrase into broad use with their 1985 federally funded study, "Mass Murder: America's Growing Menace," which they later published as a book. (They were early users of the four-or-more definition.) After analyzing more than 350 cases from 1976 to 1985—including marquee killers like Son of Sam, Ted Bundy, and Charles Manson—they suggested that aging Baby Boomers and increasing American rootlessness were harbingers of the "growing menace" of their study's title. They also suggested that most mass murderers "are basically typical, ordinary citizens and not the lunatics portrayed in movies."

"Analyses of the mass murder cases have toned down the image of a psychotic who suddenly runs amok," Fox said in a 1988 newspaper interview. "In 75 percent of the cases, the victims knew their killer, almost always a white male who often planned the killings for weeks."

The researchers explored a question still urgently asked after each new mass killing: How can they be predicted? They cited four indicators that are not so different from Birmingham's Professor Yardley's "five commonalities" (see page 17): familiarity with guns; a precipitating event, such as a divorce or a job loss; a buildup of frustration over menial employment and real or imagined insults; and isolation from friends and family who might vent the prospective killer's growing rage. But as Fox told the newsman in 1988:

There are thousands of people who fit the profile of a mass murderer, but that doesn't mean they are going to commit mass murder. In hindsight we can say "this person fits the profile," but there is no way we can tell who is going to kill.

Failed Farmer's Revenge

That certainly would have applied to Andrew Kehoe, an unlikely prototype of the American "superkiller," as the press dubbed him. Like many others, Fox and Levin have suggested that 1966 was "the onset of the age of mass murder." That was the year of two cases that stunned the nation: Richard Speck's rape and murder of eight student nurses in Chicago in July, and Charles Whitman's assault from atop the University of Texas tower just two weeks later.

But mass killings have occurred periodically in the U.S., going back much earlier—even well before a 1949 case that others often cite as a reference point. On September 6 that year, a glum gay man named Howard Unruh wandered through his Camden, New Jersey, neighborhood, firing pistol shots at anyone who crossed his path. He killed 13 people—and spent the rest of his long life in a psychiatric asylum, dying in 2009 at age 88. Doctors diagnosed him as a paranoid schizophrenic, and, like many contemporary mass killers, he felt picked on. "They have been making derogatory remarks about my character," Unruh explained to the police.

Two decades before Unruh acted out, Andrew Kehoe, an irascible type who dressed meticulously and neurotically

Twenty-seven-year-old World War II veteran Howard Unruh after police forced him from his house with tear gas. He killed 13 on the streets of Camden, New Jersey.

changed his clothes if they got dirty, set a high bar for American barbarity. Born seven years after the Civil War ended, he was approaching old age by the time ignominy came knocking in 1927. The native Michigander had always been an odd man—miserly and fussy, judgmental and stubborn, antisocial and joyless. He had studied at Michigan's State Agricultural College, and then settled just west of the East Lansing school in the small town of Bath, where his wife, Nellie, had kin. In 1918, the childless couple sold their small farm and agreed to pay Nellie's aunt $12,000 for a 185-acre spread at the edge of Bath, but within four years the farm was failing, and Nellie was bedridden with tuberculosis. The aunt held a $6,000 mortgage, and she was threatening to declare default over Kehoe's late payments.

Extensive Preparations

In 1922, Bath Township had consolidated its scattered small schools into a new central school, a durable two-story brick edifice topped with a handsome white cupola, a cherry on a sundae. The new school was a point of pride and a sign of progress for most citizens of Bath, but Andrew Kehoe hated that place. Voters had approved a property tax increase to fund its construction, and Kehoe's tax bill had spiked by $75 in 1923—another line in the red on his financial ledger. Motivated by anger, he was elected to the Bath school board on a promise of frugality, and emerged as the resident gadfly, often bickering with superintendent Emory Huyck about penny-ante school operating costs, including maintenance. In the fall of 1926, Kehoe suggested that the board could save money by appointing him the school's handyman. His colleagues agreed, and Kehoe went to work.

By the spring of 1927, he was spending most evenings at school, disappearing for hours into the bowels of the building. No one bothered to ask what he was up to, but that would soon become clear: He was fixing to bring down the schoolhouse. Crawling around like a rat, Kehoe planted dynamite beneath the classroom floorboards, rigging more than 1,000 pounds (450 kg) of dynamite and military-surplus Pyrotol, all connected by a half-mile snake of electrical wire leading to a ticking clock.

He enacted his demented plan on the morning of May 17, 1927, as the school year was ending. First of all, he bludgeoned his wife Nellie to death at home, and then he strung more wire, dynamite, and firebombs around his house and outbuildings, securing livestock so they would perish in the inferno. Early the next morning, a beautiful spring day, he packed his truck with more dynamite and drove into town. Kehoe was the first customer at the Bath Post Office, where he mailed a letter to a school board colleague. As the clock ticked down on his ghastly plan to level the school with scores of children inside, he had taken the time to write a torturously detailed note about a 22-cent error in the school's finances.

Day of Carnage

Leaving the Post Office, Kehoe passed children and teachers streaming toward the school on that Wednesday morning. He then drove back home and, at 8:45 a.m., detonated the bombs that leveled every building, destroyed every piece of machinery, and killed every animal at his farmstead—ensuring that Nellie's aunt would get nothing but the land itself. As the fire brigade rushed to Kehoe's place, a separate explosion in town shook the ground with such force that some witnesses fell to their knees to prepare for Armageddon. Bath Consolidated School had blown up, the entire left wing brought down by the colossal blast.

Parents and rescuers scrambled through the ruins, digging with bare hands to free children who could be heard moaning, but Kehoe was not yet finished. As the rescue began, he drove up in his dynamite-rigged truck and beckoned to Superintendent Huyck. When the man drew near, Kehoe detonated the vehicle bombs, killing himself, Huyck, and two others. In all, he exterminated 38 children and seven adults. Another 61 were hurt. And it could have been worse. A quarter-ton of dynamite and Pyrotol concealed under the school's right wing had failed to explode. The madman had hoped to level the entire school, not just half, and kill more than 100 innocents—all in protest of a $75 tax increase.

On May 21, 1927, after killing his wife and dynamiting his farm (its remains are pictured here), farmer Andrew Kehoe blew up Bath school and detonated his car outside it, murdering 45 people, most of them children.

What Made Kehoe a Superkiller?

Shortly after the bombings, Ohio's *Toledo Blade* newspaper posed a couple of pertinent questions: "What queer streak in his makeup made him plan with demonic cunning the dynamiting of a school filled with small children? What caused Kehoe to be a superkiller?" The answers were not forthcoming, but Andrew Kehoe did leave behind a terse not-my-fault message on a thin piece of clapboard wedged into wire fencing on his farm property. Using a stencil, he had meticulously painted his message in black across the center of the whitewashed board: "Criminals are made, not born." It was his five-word manifesto.

Scientists analyzed Kehoe's brain, and a state commission examined his crime and the events leading up to it. But there was no epiphany on the essential question of what makes an angry failed farmer commit mass murder. Levin and Fox pondered the same dilemma in the 1980s, and the search for an answer continues today. I don't know what triggers a superkiller, but I can say that the themes of despair and comeuppance have cropped up often in the obscure archival murder cases that I have explored.

Early Random Shooter

For example, there was Gilbert Twigg, a 35-year-old ex-soldier who in the summer of 1903 used a shotgun loaded with deadly double-aught buckshot to randomly attack people attending a summer band concert in Winfield, Kansas (pop. 6,000). Twigg was an early template for the nihilistic lone gunman who targets random strangers. Born in Maryland, he followed an uncle west to the Kansas town, which was best known for its largest employer, the State Asylum for Idiotic and Imbecile Youth. Perhaps the facility somehow rubbed off on Twigg. He was said to be intelligent and passably handsome, with searing ice-blue eyes obscured by spectacles to correct nearsightedness, but he went into an emotional spiral when his courtship of a young Winfield woman, Jessie Hamilton, went sour. She had accepted his marriage proposal, then abruptly rescinded after some misty incident that he later described as "little" but that she clearly regarded as big.

Abandoning his career as a miller, Twigg joined the Army to escape the town, apparently never intending to return. But after a military hitch abroad and a few years spent in Great Falls, Montana, he returned to Winfield in May 1902—still pining for Hamilton, who by then was married and raising a family up the road in Wichita. He spent his days alone in his boarding house room or lolling in a town park, convinced—like so many mass killers—that the world was rigged against him. "The boys around town commonly referred to him as 'Crazy' Twigg," the *Winfield Courier* later reported, "but no one thought he was dangerous." He proved them dead wrong.

Killer Calmly Reloaded

On August 1, 1903 Twigg visited Winfield & Miller, a hardware store, and bought a double-barrel shotgun, a .32-caliber pistol, and more than 100 rounds of ammunition. Twelve days later, he placed his armaments in a child's tin wagon, donned a buckskin hunting jacket, and waited in an alley until the townspeople had gathered for a weekly concert on a bandstand at the small city's main crossroads. At 9 p.m., in an interlude after the brass band's third song, he stepped out of the alley, dropped to one knee, and commenced firing, emptying one barrel in the direction of the bandstand, then swiveling 90 degrees and touching off the second toward the crowd.

As bodies crumpled and revelers bolted in panic, Twigg calmly reloaded and emptied his barrels three times. Men rushed him, but he dropped them with buckshot. In all, his pellets found the flesh of some 40 people, from wealthy merchants to town paupers—a drummer in the band, a farmer, a plasterer, a barber, a schoolboy. After five minutes, Crazy Twigg set down the 12-gauge and grabbed his six-shooter from the wagon, pointing it toward his face and yanking the trigger. He had killed nine innocent people—and now joined them in the hereafter.

"MADMAN'S AWFUL WORK," bellowed the front page of the *Winfield Daily Free Press*. "Streets of the City Flow with the Blood of His Many Victims."

Letter of Explanation

Twigg left a letter of explanation in his room. It was understated and gauzy by today's tell-all measures, but more than a century ago he had something in common with today's mass killers: He felt ogled and picked on:

> *I would like to say to those who have interested themselves*
> *so much in my welfare (that seems to be the public in*
> *general) that I do not and most likely never will know the*
> *real cause of being treated in the manner in which I have*

been treated . . . If I was sure that it came from the girl affair, I would go into details and tell everything, but as I am not sure and have no way to find out, I will keep it for her sake . . .

. . . Of course, you people who have been deeply interested know the way you have treated me. You know you "doped" me until I was forced to give up a $100 a month position. You know that you drove me from place to place in the same manner and forced me to give up a neat little sum of my hard-earned money to railroad companies . . . You also know that you watched my mail and after finding out my friends and correspondents, you told them some kind of a story about me that caused every one of them to drop me and turn me down cold.

. . . I have given up positions, I have taken your dope, I have taken your insults, and I have done nothing. But you will find me there delivering the goods in the end. You should let this be a lesson to you in the future . . . I believe this is all I have to say, so adios.—Gilbert

Although he addressed his note to the Winfielders, his ex-fiancée seemed to be the intended target.

Parallels with Contemporary Killers

Though written by a 1903 killer, the narrative thread of mansplaining links Twigg's "lesson"—and Kehoe's "killers are made" bromide, for that matter—to any number of I-told-you-so missives from contemporary homicidal males. "Fuckers shouldn't have ripped on me so much, huh?" said Columbine's Eric Harris, while Luke Woodham, the Mississippi human-and-dog-killer, wrote: "This world has shit on me for the final time." And on a videotape, Virginia Tech killer Seung-Hui Cho spat this message at viewers:

> *You sadistic snobs. I may be nothing but a piece of dogshit. You have vandalized my heart, raped my soul, and torched my conscience. You thought it was one pathetic boy's life you were extinguishing. Thanks to you, I die like Jesus Christ, to inspire generations of the weak and defenseless people.*

It took Andrew Kehoe 55 years on Earth to build up his murderous rage, and Twigg was pushing middle age when he blew his stack. But Cho was a young man, and Woodham and Harris were teenagers.

Wrath of a 12-Year-Old

Another overlooked member of that club of resentment, Jose Reyes, stands apart for acting out on his simmering wrath just as he arrived at puberty. He was a 12-year-old seventh-grader in 2013 when he killed a teacher and wounded two classmates at his Sparks, Nevada, middle school. Reyes, who committed suicide to conclude his attack, left two striking notes, handwritten in block lettering in a spiral school notebook. In an apologetic message addressed to his parents, he blamed the shooting on "past causes," but specifically said bullying was not a motivation.

He wrote:

> *There were some bad things in the past cause of me. And now I'm just a monster . . . When I die I will go back to the past and fix everything so it can be a great past. And the shooting of Sparks Middle School never should have happened. I wish I can be a smart and better kid so I can be the better son in our family. But if you hate me and my family doesn't love me, it's okay. I know that I'm just an idiot.*

The tone of his second note, addressed to his teachers and classmates, was angry and contradictive of the first. He wrote:

> *Today is the day when I kill you bastards for the embarrassment that you did. You say mean things in school. That I'm gay, that I'm lazy, stupid, idiot, and also say that I pee my pants and also stealing my money. Well that all ends. Today I will get revenge on the students and teachers for ruining my life. Today I will bring a god damn pistol and rifle to shoot you and see how you like it when someone [is] making fun of you. . . Have a great death at school.*

How does a child of 12 nurture such violent resentment? His reproductive hardware may contain the answer. In the late 1980s, the Australian sociologist Raewyn Connell coined the term "hegemonic masculinity" in her textbook *Gender and*

Power, a key title in the women's studies canon. It is defined as "a practice that legitimizes men's dominant position in society and justifies the subordination of women." Subsequently, other researchers have linked hegemonic masculinity—or the related "toxic masculinity"—to mass shooters. "The culture of hegemonic masculinity in the US creates a sense of aggrieved entitlement conducive to violence," writes New York sociologist Rachel Kalish. "This sense of entitlement simultaneously frames suicide as an appropriate, instrumental behavior for these males to underscore their violent enactment of masculinity."

So that brings us back to the essential question: What makes a superkiller? Testosterone, for one thing. When males like Twigg, Kehoe, Unruh, Harris, Cho, and Reyes feel shamed and emasculated, they are driven to exact revenge, however over the top their response might seem. As Kalish explains: "Violence is restorative, compensatory."

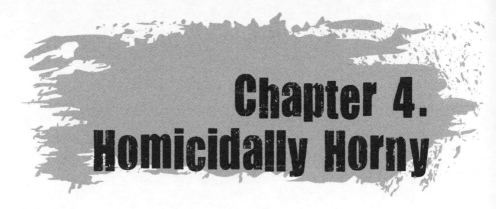

Chapter 4.
Homicidally Horny

On Christmas Eve 2008, a desperately lonely George Sodini sat at his computer in a Pittsburgh, Pennsylvania, suburb and puzzled over his sexless life. "Moving into Christmas again," Sodini wrote in his online diary. "No girlfriend since 1984 . . . Who knows why. I am not ugly or too weird. No sex since July 1990 . . . Over 18 years ago." Sodini, 48 years old, was bewildered by this fate. He saw himself as a catch because he was fit, handsome enough, and had gleaming bleached teeth. His financial assets, including a new Nissan automobile, a small house, and modest investments, totaled nearly $250,000, and his job as a law firm IT tech afforded him money to spare. But he had no love to spend it on. Five days later, he returned to his journal to peer deeper into his loneliness:

> *Just got back from tanning, been doing this for a while . . . I actually look good. I dress good, am clean-shaven, bathe, touch of cologne—yet 30 million women rejected me—over an 18- or 25-year period. That is how I see it. Thirty*

million is my rough guesstimate of how many desirable single women there are . . . A man needs a woman for confidence . . . Flying solo for many years is a destroyer. Yet many people say I am easy to get along with, etc.

George Sodini felt rejected. He saw himself as a catch because he was fit, handsome enough and had gleaming bleached teeth. Yet he couldn't get a girlfriend...

Looking back, I owe nothing to desirable females who ask for anything, except for basic courtesy—usually. Looking back over everything, what bothers me most is the inability to work towards whatever change I choose.

The Involuntary Celibate

In the mass shooting canon, George Sodini is cited as a prototype of the homicidally angry "involuntary celibate," or incel. Many of these men see themselves as a subset tribe of the downtrodden. They gather online and exchange complaints in their own language, often with themes drawn from the hagiographic writings of men like Sodini and Elliot Rodger, the suicidal virgin who rampaged against young women in 2014 in Isla Vista, California. Before he acted out, Rodger produced an extraordinarily self-absorbed, 100,000-word misogynist screed that detailed dozens of perceived petty affronts by females, an onslaught that began, by his account, when he was barely ambulatory. His autobiography begins melodramatically and never strays:

> *All of my suffering in this world has been at the hands of humanity, particularly women . . . All I ever wanted was to fit in and live a happy life amongst humanity, but I was cast out and rejected, forced to endure an existence of loneliness and insignificance, all because the females of the human species were incapable of seeing the value in me . . . This is the story of my entire life. It is a dark story of sadness, anger, and hatred. It is*

*a story of a war against cruel injustice . . . This tragedy
did not have to happen. I didn't want things to turn out
this way, but humanity forced my hand, and this story
will explain why . . .*

As we will see in the next chapter, his attempt at explanation falls short, but a growing number of contemporary mass murderers inspired or motivated by misogyny have aligned themselves with Rodger's club of incel killers. Among this lonesome, loathsome clan is Alek Minassian, a socially inept Canadian who used a rented van in April 2018 to run down more than two dozen pedestrians along bustling Yonge Street in the Toronto suburb of North York. He killed ten people and tried to end his life with suicide-by-cop, begging to be shot dead—increasingly, the endgame goal of most mass killers. An officer arrested him instead.

Minassian's crimes brought new attention to this simmering substrate of mutant masculinity. On his Facebook page just before the murders, Minassian tipped his hat to an "incel rebellion," as though it were something new, but in fact its roots are primeval. Lonely-hearted men for centuries have used sexual rejection as a murder motive.

Fight Against Feminism

For example, there was Marc Lépine. On an icy December evening in 1989, the crazed Canadian burst into a classroom at Ecole Polytechnique, the engineering school at the University of Montreal. He fired a warning shot into the ceiling, then separated the 60 students by gender—"girls to the left, guys to the right."

After allowing the 51 men to leave, he turned toward the huddled women and asked whether they knew why he was there. No, they stammered. "I'm here to fight against feminism," he announced. He then leveled his Ruger Mini-14 assault rifle at the defenseless women and fired as many as 30 rounds, chasing down those who scrambled for cover under desks.

Six of the nine women were killed and the other three were seriously wounded. After that he stalked out of Room 230 and marched along the school corridors, firing at more women as he made his way to a cafeteria, packed with nearly 100 students, where he shot four women. Moving to another room, he killed two more. He then went up an escalator to the third floor and found another class in Room 311, where he shot a female student who was leading a presentation. He moved relentlessly up and down the room's aisle, firing at women cowered behind desks but sparing men. Lépine returned to the front of the room, drew a knife and stabbed the wounded woman presenter. He then sat down, removed his cap, and blew his brains out.

Lépine killed 14 women and wounded ten others. (Four men also were injured.) In many ways, he wrote the script for the alienated, suicidal, misogynist mass killers to come. He had two beefs: He couldn't get a date, and he believed women had no business studying engineering. Canadians were stupefied. This was the sort of violence that was supposed to happen in the United States, not Canada.

The government spent months investigating where it had gone wrong with Lépine, the son of an abusive Algerian immigrant father and a French-Canadian mother. He was a socially awkward, below-average student who resented the menial jobs he was forced to work when he flunked out of college, and he somehow blamed women for this. His festering rage erupted when he was rejected by the engineering school. In the killer's pocket police found a rambling rant—handwritten in French—in which Lépine tried to rationalize his irrational act. Note his reference to the "advantages" bestowed upon women. Some excerpts:

> *Would you note that if I commit suicide today 89-12-06 it is not for economic reasons (for I have waited until I exhausted all my financial means, even refusing jobs) but for political reasons. Because I have decided to send the feminists, who have always ruined my life, to their maker. For seven years life has brought me no joy and being totally blasé, I have decided to put an end to those viragos . . .*
>
> *Being rather backward-looking by nature (except for science), the feminists have always enraged me. They want to keep the advantages of women (e.g. cheaper insurance, extended maternity leave preceded by a preventative leave, etc.) while seizing for themselves those of men.*
>
> *. . . They are so opportunistic they [do not] neglect to profit from the knowledge accumulated by men through the ages. They always try to misrepresent them every time they can. Thus, the other day, I heard they were honoring the Canadian men and women who*

fought at the frontline during the world wars. How can
you explain [that since] women were not authorized to
go to the frontline??? . . . A real Casus Belli.

Like so many mass killers who have left a written record, Lépine wanted to assure his readers that he was perfectly sane—even if the evidence suggested otherwise: "Even if the Mad Killer epithet will be attributed to me by the media, I consider myself a rational erudite that only the arrival of the Grim Reaper has forced to take extreme acts."

Anger at Sexual Rejection

The masculine toxicity of George Sodini, Pittsburgh's Mr. Lonelyhearts, seemed less panoramic by comparison. His anger was centered on sexual rejection, not the broader female "advantages" that Lépine saw through his warped lens. In his journal, Sodini traced his women troubles to his own family—an inattentive father, a domineering mother, and an older brother whom he blamed for sabotaging his relationships. He described his father and brother as "useless" in offering advice that might help him hook up. And this was his journal's thumbnail profile of his mother:

Mum—The Central Boss . . . Don't piss her off or she will
be mad and vindictive for years. She actually thinks she's
normal. Very dominant. Her way and only her way with
no flexibility toward everyone in the household. A power
and control thing. People outside the immediate family

like her. Why are people vicious with their closest ones?
She is the Boss above all other Bosses.

Elliot Rodger's long autobiography suggests that he made few attempts to resolve the "cruel injustice" of his sexlessness, rarely working up the gumption to so much as speak to a woman, let alone date. Sodini, on the other hand, was out there actively trying to fix his deficiencies, even though he made an unfortunate choice of one relationship exemplar.

Sex Counseling

He became an acolyte of R. Don Steele, a throwback counselor from California who mansplains the mysteries of women with all the subtlety of a drill sergeant. Known as "Steel Balls," he bills his strategies as "Time-Tested Dating Principles for Men." Much of his advice seems ripped from a soft-porn romance novel penned by a Neanderthal. His website includes a step-by-step primer on snaring a "dream girl." Sodini bought Steele's how-to book, and early in 2008 he traveled to Los Angeles to attend the author's three-day, eight-hour seminar. Sodini appears a number of times in a video of the gathering, which included about two dozen men and several young women—"Titanium Babes," in Steele's term—who were paid to offer expert gender testimony. On the video, Steele begins by writing "NICE GUY MUST DIE" on a whiteboard. He tells the assembled men: "I would say that's the problem with most of the guys in the room—that you're too nice. Women don't like that. They don't respect it. It's about as arousing as a booger." Steele surely struck a chord with

Sodini by suggesting that many men must overcome emotional wounding by their own mothers:

> *It's normal to be scared when you have been hurt by women in the past. The first woman who hurts you is your mother. And that lasts a lifetime . . . Some women are crazy, and they deliberately hurt their children. But most of us don't have mothers like that. Some of us do. But most of us who do know that mother was crazy. It really wasn't my fault. That doesn't make the pain any less. That doesn't make you any less afraid of women, but it makes it understandable . . .*

He had this macho advice for any tender souls in the room: "If you've had one heartbreak, my attitude is, oh, too fuckin' bad, you pussy. Suck it up. C'mon, get back in the game."

Self-Made Videos

As "homework" from the seminar, Sodini uploaded online at least two self-made videos. The first was a four-minute tour of his house, intended to show he was a man of means with a nest ready for a potential mate. Sodini began:

> *This is a two-bedroom brick ranch, conveniently located. I paid $79,000 for this in '06. That's considered a lot, believe it or not . . . Inside, OK, here's my big-screen TV, 32 inch. My computer . . . The couch and chair, they match. The woman will really be impressed . . . My bedroom . . .*

Looks pretty clean. I'm sure she'll be impressed . . . The kitchen, stove and counters, everything I need . . . Well, that about sums it up.

Another 74-second video shows Sodini standing in his cellar in front of a punching bag, delivering a stiff message about his resolution to be more emotionally available. "It is easy for me to hide from my emotions for one more day," he says. "My objective is to be real and to learn to be emotional and to be able to emotionally connect with people." Citing Steele's advice, Sodini continues haltingly (and confusingly) with references to "STEM exercises or forgiveness exercises" that he apparently believed would help nurture a relationship with the younger women he desired. "Because when I'm ten to 20 years older than she is, you know, she has to feel good about this thing," he says. A few seconds later, he awkwardly ends by saying: "I'm gonna post this and see what comes back." He then steps away from the camera.

It seems unlikely that any woman—let alone the "desirable" young hotties he mooned over—would reply to either video. They are humorless and reveal no personality or magnetism— certainly not Steel Balls' no more Mr. Nice Guy. George Sodini comes off as a sincere but graceless and rather sad man. His journal jeremiads hearken to Travis Bickle, the depressed, insomniac cabbie portrayed by Robert De Niro in *Taxi Driver*, Martin Scorsese's 1976 neo-noir film set in gritty New York.

"Loneliness has followed me my whole life, everywhere," Bickle says. "In bars, in cars, sidewalks, stores, everywhere. There's no escape. I'm God's lonely man."

Chickens Out of First Attempt

Sodini was still alone on New Year's Eve 2008, and he had abandoned whatever optimism he must have had when he produced the Steele-inspired videos. He typed another note into his journal that night, hinting at a dark impending ending:

> *My dad never (not once) talked to me or asked about my life's details and tell me what he knew. He was just a useless sperm donor . . . Brother was actually counterproductive and would try to embarrass me or discourage my efforts when pursuing things, esp girls early on (teen years). Useless bully. Result is I am learning basics by trial and error in my 40s, followed by discouragement. Seems odd, but that's true. Writing all this is helping me justify my plan and to see the futility of continuing. Too embarrassed to tell anyone this, at almost 50 one is expected to just know these things.*

In *Taxi Driver*, Travis Bickle rages about his monotonous life and his impotence to change it: "The days go on and on. They don't end . . . Over and over, one day indistinguishable from the next. A long continuous chain." Engulfed in an existential crisis, Sodini channeled Bickle again in a January 5, 2009, journal entry:

> *No matter how many changes I try to make, things stay the same. Every evening I am alone, and then go to bed alone. Young women were brutal when I was younger, now they aren't as much, probably because they just see me just as*

another old man . . . I think those years slipped right by
for me. Why should I continue another 20+ years alone? I
will just work, come home, eat, maybe do something, then
go to bed (alone) for the next day of the same thing. This
is the Auschwitz Syndrome, to be in serious pain so long
one thinks it is normal. I cannot wait for tomorrow!

He had resolved to enact an "exit plan" the next day: Armed with several handguns, he would barge into his fitness center, shoot as many women as he could, then commit suicide. Here are his diary entries for that day, January 6, 2009:

I can do this. Leaving work today, I felt like a zombie—
just going thru the motions. Get on the bus, get the
car, drive home . . . My mind is screwed up anymore, I
can't concentrate at work or think at all. This log is not
detailed. It is only for confidence to do this. The future
holds even less than what I have today.

   It is 6:40 p.m., about hour and a half to go. God have
mercy. I wish life could be better for all and the crazy world
can somehow run smoother. I wish I had answers. Bye.

   It is 8:45 p.m. I chickened out! Shit! I brought the
loaded guns, everything. Hell!

Sodini's life seemed to improve over the ensuing months. Amid the country's economic meltdown, he survived an April 2009 layoff at the Pittsburgh law firm where he worked as a computer technician, he had a date with a woman in May, and he was awarded both a promotion and a salary raise in July. But he could never escape his own gloomy shadow. By May 2009, he had again begun planning an exit.

Journal Excerpts Prior to Shooting:

MAY 4

I know I will never enjoy life. This is an over 30-year trend. Some people are happy, some are miserable. It is difficult to live almost continuously feeling an undercurrent of fear, worry, discontentment and helplessness . . . I am making a list of items that will provide motivation to do the exit plan . . . I made many big changes in the past two years, but everything is still the same. Life is over . . .

MAY 18

I actually had a date today. It was with a woman I met on the bus in March. We got together at Two PPG Place for lunch. The last date for me was May 1, 2008. Women just don't like me. There are 30 million desirable women in the US (my estimate) and I cannot find one. Not one of them finds me attractive . . . Makes me realize how TOTALLY ALONE, a deeper word is ISOLATED, I am from all else. I no longer have any expectations of myself. I have no options because I cannot work toward and achieve even the smallest goals. That is, ABOVE ALL, what bothers me the most. Not to be able to work towards what I want in my life.

MAY 29

Another lonely Friday night, I'm done. This is too much.

JUNE 2

Some people I was talking with believed I date a lot and get around with women. They think this because I showed an email I got from a hot woman to the department gossip, but it didn't work out. All this is funny. Actually, I haven't had sex since I was 29 years old, 19 years ago. That's true.

JULY 20

Everything still sucks. But I got a promotion and a raise, even in this shitty Obama economy . . . But that is NOT what I want in life . . . I have slept alone for over 20 years. Last time I slept all night with a girlfriend it was 1982. Proof I am a total malfunction. Girls and women don't even give me a second look ANYWHERE. There is something BLATANTLY wrong with me that NO goddam person will tell me what it is. Every person just wants to be fucking nice and say nice things to me. Flattery. Oh yeah, I am sure you can get a date anytime. You look good, etc. Pussies . . .

JULY 23

Wow!! I just looked out my front window and saw a beautiful college-age girl leave [name redacted]'s house, across the street. I guess he got a good lay today. College girls are hoez. I masturbate. Frequently. He is about 45 years old. She was a long haired, hot little hottie with a beautiful bod . . . I have masturbated since age 13. Thanks, mum and brother (by blood alone). And dad, old man, for TOTALLY ignoring me through the years. All of you DEEPLY helped me be this way.

AUGUST 3

I took off today, Monday, and tomorrow to practice my routine and make sure it is well polished. I need to work out every detail, there is only one shot . . . Tomorrow is the big day . . . Last time I tried this, in January, I chickened out. Let's see how this new approach works.

Maybe soon, I will see God and Jesus . . . I was reading the Bible and The Integrity of God [a book by R.B. Thieme Jr.] beginning yesterday, because soon I will see them . . .

Maybe all this will shed insight on why some people just cannot make things happen in their life, which can potentially benefit others.

Deadly Aerobics Class

He did not chicken out the second time, on August 4. At 11 that morning he visited his gym, LA Fitness in suburban Pittsburgh, for a walk-through, returning nine hours later with several handguns in a gym bag. He paused outside to phone his mother, then entered at 8 p.m., as a women's aerobics dance class began.

Thirty women had assembled for a fun, rousing workout. Sodini stepped into their room at 8:15, switched off the lights, drew a pair of Glock semi-automatic pistols and began shooting. He squeezed off about 50 shots, hitting a dozen women. Three were killed: Jody Billingsley, 38, Elizabeth Gannon, 49, and Heidi Overmier, 46. Sodini then shot himself in the head. He was trying to untangle his knotted id to the very end. This was his final diary entry: "Probably 99% of the people who know me well don't even think I was this crazy. Told by at least 100 girls/ women over the years I was a 'nice guy.' Not kidding."

Notes he left echoed his journal's themes, and this record of laments has bestowed post-mortem celebrity on Sodini, as a wounded soul among incels. But the appropriate exclamation point to his pathetic life was a macho provocation he wrote in his journal on June 5, 2009, two months before his rampage:

> I was reading several posts on different forums and it seems many teenage girls have sex frequently. One 16-year-old does it usually three times a day with her boyfriend. So, err, after a month of that, this little hoe has had more sex than ME in my LIFE, and I am 48. One more reason. Thanks for nada, bitches! Bye.

Eric Harris's Rape-Fantasy

Misogyny is the connecting tissue of many mass killers, including some who are not necessarily considered part of the involuntary celibates' club. For example, there is this rape-fantasy and cannibalism riff from the journal of Columbine's Eric Harris. He wrote it in November 1998, five months before his massacre:

> *You know what—maybe I just need to get laid. Maybe that'll just change some shit around. That's another thing, I am a fucking dog. I have fantasies of just taking someone and fucking them hard and strong. Someone like where I just pick her up, take her to my room, tear off her shirt and pants and just eat her out and fuck her hard. I love flesh . . . weisses fleisch!* [In German, white flesh.]
>
> *Dein weisses fleisch erregt mich so, Ich bin doch nur ein Gigolo!* ["Your white flesh excites me so, I am just a gigolo"—from a song by Rammstein, a German band. The first two lines of the song, translated, are: "You in the schoolyard/ I am ready to kill"]. *I want to grab a few different girls in my gym class, take them into a room, pull their pants off and fuck them hard . . . Call it teenager hormones or call it a crazy fuckin racist rapist. Es ist mir egal.* [It's all the same to me.]

Five months later, he had failed in his quest for consummation. This was the final entry in his journal, from April 3, 1999, two weeks before the attack. Like Elliot Rodger and George Sodini, Harris was baffled by his sexless fate.

> *Right now I'm trying to get fucked and trying to finish off these time bombs. NBK* [Natural Born Killers, his name

for their planned attack] *came quick. Why the fuck can't I get any? I mean, I'm nice and considerate and all that shit, but nooooo. I think I try too hard. But I kinda need to considering NBK is closing in . . . I hate you people for leaving me out of so many fun things. And no don't fucking say, "Well that's your fault" because it isn't, you people had my phone #, and I asked and all, but no. No no no don't let the weird-looking Eric KID come along, ohh fucking nooo.*

Maybe it was his misogyny and racism, traits he shared with other homicidally horny men.

Killers' Racist Rants

GEORGE SODINI

George Sodini's very first journal entry, on November 5, 2008, begins with a racist rant suggesting that the election of President Obama the day before would allow black men access to the young white women that Sodini salivated over:

Good luck to Obama! He will be successful. The liberal media LOVES him. Amerika has chosen The Black Man. Good! In light of this I got ideas outside of Obama's plans for the economy and such. Here it is: Every black man should get a young white girl hoe to hone up on. Kinda a reverse indentured servitude thing. Long ago, many an older white male landowner had a young Negro wench girl for his desires. 'Bout time tables are turned on that shit. Besides, dem young white hoez dig da bruthrs! LOL. More so than they dig the white dudes! Every daddy know when he sends his little girl to college, she be bangin a bruthr real good . . . Black dudes have their choice of best white hoez. You do the math, there are enough young whites so all the brothers can each have one for 3 or 6 months or so.

ELLIOT RODGER

Interracial romance is a common trigger for white incels. A racist passage in Elliot Rodger's autobiography has become a bugle call for sexless white men. Curiously, Rodger was of mixed racial background, with a white British father and an Asian mother. He wrote about a crying jag that followed a conversation with his sexually active college roommates:

My first week turned out to be very unpleasant, leaving a horrific first impression of my new life in Santa Barbara. My two housemates were nice, but they kept inviting over this friend of theirs named Chance. He was a black boy who came over all the time, and I hated his cocksure attitude . . . I was eating a meal in the kitchen when he came over and started bragging to my housemates about his success with girls . . . I couldn't stand it, so I proceeded to ask them all if they were virgins. They all looked at me weirdly and said that they had lost their virginity long ago. I felt so inferior . . . And then . . . Chance said that he lost his virginity when he was only thirteen! In addition, he said that the girl he lost his virginity to was a blonde white girl! . . . I indignantly told him that I did not believe him, and then I went to my room to cry.

How could an inferior, ugly black boy be able to get a white girl and not me? I am beautiful, and I am half white myself. I am descended from British aristocracy. He is descended from slaves . . . If this is actually true, if this ugly black filth was able to have sex with a blonde white girl at the age of thirteen while I've had to suffer virginity all my life, then this just proves how ridiculous the female gender is. They would give themselves to this filthy scum, but they reject ME? The injustice!

CHRISTOPHER HARPER-MERCER

Seventeen months after Rodger's rampage, another suicidal virgin paid homage to the Californian's racism in his own manifesto. Chris Harper-Mercer, who shot and killed nine people and himself in 2015 at his Roseburg, Oregon, community college, left behind 1,600 words of musing and explanation, including this comment: "Elliot Rodger was right when he said his thoughts on the black male. I fully agree with him." Nearly one-third of Harper-Mercer's document is a section entitled "Blackness and its effect on men," in which he characterizes black men as hypersexual beasts. This is strange since his mother, Laurel Harper, was black. (On the day of the shooting, Harper told the police: "I mean, he was born angry, pretty much. I mean, even the doctor said this is one angry baby.")

The ideas sketched in the roughly 100 sentences that constitute Harper-Mercer's manifesto could keep a Freudian analyst engaged for years. Harper was obsessed with the black penis, for one thing. As the African-American scholar Houston A. Baker has noted, the black phallus is "a symbol of unconstrained force that white men contradictorily envy and seek to destroy." That applies to the mixed-race Harper-Mercer, as well. He suggests castration of black men:

> When the girls would rather go with alpha thug black men, we can all agree that something's wrong with the world. When good individuals like myself are alone, but wicked black men get the loot, like some sort of vaginal pirate, it's not fair.
>
> . . . But don't take these words to be racist. I don't hate blacks. Just the men. Now of course some of you will be saying, wait, you're 40% black aren't you? Ah yes dear reader, I am, but thankfully my partial blackness didn't come from a man. If it had, my brain would have been fried. It is the black male who is foolish . . .
>
> Black men have corrupted the women of this planet. All they care about is sex and swag. All they care about is swinging their "BBC thang" around in public. All their brain power has been submerged into their penis . . . The black woman can only be saved by the castration/ elimination of the black man . . .

Not all mass killers have left a record of overt racism, but many have. And it seems more than coincidence that the black phallus arises as an object of contemplation in the leavings of the marquee names among the incel mass shooters.

Chapter 5.
The "Magnificent Gentleman"

Although the point likely was lost on the narcissistic author, Elliot Rodger's book-length jeremiad about his deep loneliness serves as a manifest exhibit not only of his tortured sexlessness but also of the personal failings that placed him in that condition.

Beyond its passable prose, there is little to admire in Rodger's long self-portrait. I can't cite a single passage in his 100,000-word tome that might engender a reader's empathy. He grandly entitled his hagiography *My Twisted World: The Story of Elliot Rodger*. I found a better title in a comment he made on page 95, which neatly summarizes his central theme: "I Was Highly Offended."

His repetitive, indefatigable complaints reveal an emotionally stunted man who is preening, melodramatic, entitled, hypersensitive, misogynistic, racist, and, generally, clueless. No wonder he couldn't get a date. Yet he held himself in the highest esteem, describing himself as kind, intelligent, superior, eminent, glorious, supreme, and—repeatedly—a "magnificent gentleman."

> *Turning 21 as a kissless virgin was indeed a dark day. How pathetic it was, to be 21 and still a virgin while kids were having sex at the age of 14? The unfairness of life on this world is staggeringly horrific! . . .*
>
> *I will never have sex, never have love, never have children. I will never be a creator, but I could be a destroyer. Life had been cruel to me. The human species had rejected me all my life, despite the fact that I am the ideal, magnificent gentleman. Life itself is twisted and disgusting . . . Humans are brutal animals. If I cannot thrive among them, then I will destroy them all. I didn't want things to turn out this way. I wanted a happy, healthy life of love and sex. But if I'm unable to have such a life, then I will have no choice but to exact revenge on the society that denied it to me.*

James Alan Fox, the Boston criminologist, told me that he is offended when writers use "manifesto" to describe the written leavings of most mass killers, and he cited Rodger in particular. Fox argues that most of these men leave self-reverential tripe or trivial drool—like Kimveer Gill's ode to cheesy puffs. Many news stories have referred to Rodger's autobiography as a manifesto because it is so long. As Fox explained in a newspaper column:

When exactly did the angry rants of a mass murderer become rightfully characterized as a manifesto? Although Rodger's document is a manifestation of emotional disturbance, it hardly qualifies to be called a manifesto. A true manifesto reflects the political ideology of a formidable leader of men, a political force to be reckoned with. Nowhere in his 141 pages does Rodger describe his manuscript in such a way. So why should we?

I can't disagree. Of the more than 50 cases I examined of mass killers who left written or recorded thoughts, Rodger's is the most irritating. Irrational jealousy is a core theme. He uses the

Selfie time for Elliot Rodger, who was emotionally stunted, melodramatic, entitled, hypersensitive, misogynistic, racist, and, generally, clueless.

words *jealous* or *jealousy* 29 times in the document, including one fleeting moment of self-examination when he wrote: "Jealousy and envy . . . those are two feelings that would dominate my entire life and bring me immense pain."

Many other word patterns emerged in my analysis of the document, which he wrote in the final months of his life. He mentions virginity 66 times—roughly once every other page—and refers to loneliness even more often, 79 times. For example: "I had to watch beautiful young people enjoying their lives together as I languished in loneliness and despair, because no one accepted me." Many other words that are billboards for depression crop up over and over—*misery* or *miserable* 47 times; a form of *cruel* 31 times; *envy* 26 times; *bitter* or *inferior* two dozen times each, and *embarrassed* 20 times. He refers to his *shame* 16 times and *humiliation* nine times. He repeatedly calls himself "invisible" or mouse-like: "I felt like such an inferior mouse whenever I saw guys walking with beautiful girls." He used the word *depression* 28 times.

Rodger wields another favorite adjective—*heavenly*—in his frequent salacious (if conflicted) musings about how dreamy life could be if only he had a companion.

> *When a man has sex with a beautiful woman, he probably feels like he is in heaven. But the world is not supposed to be heaven. For some humans to actually be able to feel such heights of heavenly pleasure is selfish and hedonistic.*

Not that he didn't dip into self-hedonism. He admits to chronic masturbation—"at least every other day."

Narcissistic Injury

Shrinks who have examined Rodger's work say it is a textbook example of what the *Diagnostic and Statistical Manual of Mental Disorders* calls "narcissistic injury," which is defined as:

> *vulnerability in self-esteem which makes narcissistic people very sensitive to "injury" from criticism or defeat. Although they may not show it outwardly, criticism may haunt these individuals and may leave them feeling humiliated, degraded, hollow and empty. They react with disdain, rage, or defiant counterattack.*

James Garbarino, a psychology professor in Chicago, described narcissistic injury to a journalist: "It's part of a general effort to say, 'I am the center of the world and anyone who stands against me has committed a horrible outrage.'" Karyl McBride, a Denver psychologist, went deeper in her blog:

> *Narcissists swing from depression to grandiosity with little in-between . . . When the narcissists' facade of charm and deception gets cracked, their whole world bursts apart. They will blame you for their feelings of inadequacy, lack of happiness, and lack of love. When narcissists feel that they have lost or they feel rejected or abandoned, they don't forget it . . . Narcissists are not*

enough in touch with their own feelings to move on. The
issues remain in their mind as "It's all your fault." "How
could you do this to me?" They want to strike back.

Katherine Ramsland, a true crime author who teaches forensic
psychology in Pennsylvania, described the visceral reaction when
she introduced her students to Rodger through a video he made
as a companion to his autobiography.

> *When I show just five minutes of the whiny YouTube clips*
> *of mass murderer Elliot Rodger to my students, it's obvious*
> *from female reactions why this entitled narcissist had no*
> *girlfriend. Although they think he's moderately attractive*
> *physically, they find his self-pitying rants repugnant.*

Remarkably, Rodger thought that very video might get him a
date. He wrote:

> *I titled one of the videos I uploaded "Why do girls hate*
> *me so much?" in which I ask the entire population*
> *of women the question I've wanted to ask them for*
> *so many years. Why do they hate me so much? Why*
> *have they never fancied me? Why do they give their*
> *love and sex to other men, but not me, even though I*
> *deserve them more? In the video, I show that I am the*
> *perfect, magnificent gentleman, worthy of having a*
> *beautiful girlfriend . . . In fact, a small part of me was*
> *even hoping that a girl would see the video and contact*

me to give me a chance to go on a date. That alone would have prevented the Day of Retribution, if one girl had just given me one chance. But no . . . As expected, I got absolutely no response from any girls . . . This just shows how evil and sadistic they are. Oh well, they will realize the gravity of their crimes when I slaughter them all on the Day of Retribution. How dare they reject a magnificent gentleman like me!

Day of the Attack

Rodger exacted his warped revenge on May 23, 2014, in Isla Vista, California, near the Santa Barbara campus of the state university, which he had attended sporadically. His mass murder was modest by contemporary American standards, and he failed in his goal to target women and "slaughter them all." He killed six people—four of them were men—and wounded 14 others, before killing himself. His self-described Day of Retribution occurred shortly after he posted three pouty videos on YouTube—and 22 months after his 21st birthday, the "dark day" when he reached full adulthood as a kissless virgin.

After beginning his attack by stabbing to death his two male housemates and another man in his apartment, he then visited Starbucks for his daily indulgence: a triple vanilla latte. At 9:15 p.m., Rodger arrived in his black BMW coupe—a gift from his well-to-do parents—at the Alpha Phi sorority house, which to him was a symbolic hive of the tall, beautiful blond women who, in his mind, had rejected him. Fittingly, no one answered his knock, so he returned to his car and shot three women who happened to be walking by. Two were killed but the third survived.

Over the ensuing ten minutes Rodger sped helter-skelter through Isla Vista, firing shots out the car window and swerving to run down pedestrians. Police caught up when he crashed into a parked car. A half-dozen deputies fired a total of 31 shots at the BMW, but just one found its mark, wounding Rodger in the hip. He put an exclamation point on his rampage with a fatal and final self-inflicted shot to the head. As with most mass shootings, the toll could have been worse. Rodger had fired about 55 shots but police found an arsenal of 500 additional unspent rounds in his car.

Thankfully, he had also failed to follow through on one of the more appalling details of his murderous plan, lost in the focus on his incel motivations. He explains in his autobiography that spurred by a tiff with his stepmother, Soumaya, he had decided to kill his half-brother, Jazz, because he seemed destined "to surpass me at everything." The object of his jealousy was six years old. He described this epiphanic moment:

> I had an argument with Soumaya while I was visiting father's house. It started when she began to boast that my brother Jazz was recently signed by an agent to act in TV commercials. She said that by the time he is my age, he will be a successful actor. I talked about how Jazz was already so socially savvy for his age, and how I've always envied him for it. She told me he will never have

any problems with girls and will lose his virginity while he's young. I had to sit there and listen to the bitch tell me that my little brother will grow up enjoying the life I've always craved for but missed out on . . . Girls will love him. He will become one of my enemies.

That was the day that I decided I would have to kill him on the Day of Retribution . . . It will be a hard thing to do, because I had really bonded with my little brother in the last year, and he respected and looked up to me. But I would have to do it. If I can't live a pleasurable life, then neither will he! I will not let him put my legacy to shame.

Chad and Stacy Complex

In the gloomy precincts online where involuntary celibates gather to grumble and commiserate, the objects of their enmity are known as Chad and Stacy, representing the Ken-and-Barbie, jock-and-cheerleader couples that intimidate incels. Alek Minassian, a Canadian who was driven to mass homicide by his social ineptitude, mentioned the straw-man couple in a Facebook shout-out to his clan in the hours before he mowed down pedestrians on a suburban Toronto street in April 2018: "The Incel Rebellion has already begun! We will overthrow all the Chads and Stacys! All hail the Supreme Gentleman Elliot Rodger!"

But there is a thin line between antipathy and veneration. Among incels, the male partner in the confoundingly bedazzled couple is often known as Chad Thundercock. And Stacy seems to be precisely their wet-dream model. Rodger certainly was afflicted with Barbie Doll disease. He mentions blondes more than 60 times in his autobiography. It was an obsession: "I did my usual fantasizing about having sex with a beautiful, tall, blonde-haired girl . . ." He returns again to his hair-color theme in this creepy passage in which he explains how he chose one of his murder targets:

> *After doing a lot of extensive research within the last year, I found out that the sorority with the most beautiful girls is Alpha Phi Sorority . . . I've sat outside it in my car to stalk them many times. Alpha Phi sorority is full of hot, beautiful blonde girls; the kind of girls I've always desired but was never able to have because they all look down on me. They are all spoiled, heartless, wicked bitches. They think they are superior to me, and if I ever tried to ask one on a date, they would reject me cruelly. I will sneak into their house at around 9:00 p.m. on the Day of Retribution, just before all of the partying starts, and slaughter every single one of them with my guns and knives . . . Then we shall see who the superior one really is!*

Inability to Interact with Women

That encapsulates so many of Rodger's psycho-sexual problems. He sat in his car stalking these women, but "if I ever tried to ask one on a date, they would reject me cruelly." His autobiography reveals Rodger's inability to interact even nominally with women, in spite of his bellyaching about their lack of interest. According to his own account, he was never explicitly sexually rejected because he never got close enough to a woman for intimacy to become a possibility. Rodger lacked the minimal social skills needed to strike up a conversation with a woman—or even say hello—let alone sleep with her. In reality, he was petrified of women. His parents were aware of this deficiency and hired life coaches to teach him sociability, to no avail.

According to his autobiography, Rodger in the entirety of his life had perhaps a half-dozen of the most trifling interactions with women. He would get a crush on a college classmate, then end up dropping the class because, as he writes, he could not "endure the torment of watching other guys talking to the girls I liked. And then I would go home alone, open the door to my lonely room, and feel absolutely miserable." Another time, he claimed he hurled a Starbucks coffee out his car window at two girls on the street who failed to return his smile. Here is his typically hyperbolic reaction:

> *How dare those girls snub me in such a fashion. How dare they insult me so! . . . Those girls deserved to be dumped in boiling water for the crime of not giving me the attention and adoration I so rightfully deserve!*

Nearly as striking is a vignette that Rodger remarkably describes as the most euphoric episode in his life—when a woman he passed while walking on the beach in Malibu smiled at him. Yet even this moment of lightness led to a dark place:

> *On the private beach, I could enjoy the serenity of the environment without having to worry about young couples making me jealous . . . I did, however, pass by one young girl, and she was like a goddess who came down from heaven . . . She was walking alone, in her bathing suit, with her luscious blonde hair blowing in the wind. I couldn't help but slyly admire her beauty as we passed by each other . . . And then, just as we passed each other, she actually looked at me. She looked at me and smiled . . . I had never felt so euphoric in my life. One smile was all it took to brighten my entire day . . .*
>
> *That smile put me in a good, healthy mood for the rest of that walk, but it soon faded away as I realized that I could never actually have a girl as beautiful as that. She probably only smiled out of politeness . . . Some men get to have beautiful girlfriends like that, and some don't. I am among those who are denied such a pleasure, and that is why I hate life.*

Like many mass killers, Rodger wanted everyone to read his tale of woe. So he emailed copies to 34 people and places, including the media, his therapist, former teachers, old friends, and his mother and father. He hoped his "epic" life story would become a motion picture, but it wasn't much of a life; only the ending was noteworthy.

Early Life

Rodger was born in London to an English father, Peter Rodger, and a Malaysian mother, Ong Li Chin. His father worked as a motion picture photographer, and his mother was a film-set nurse. Before Elliot started school, the family moved to Los Angeles, where Peter Rodger carried on working in the film industry. (Elliot's internationalism was a point of pride: "At the age of 4, I, Elliot Rodger, had already been to six different countries. Who can claim that, eh?") His parents soon divorced, and their son shuttled between one and the other (and their partners) for the rest of his life. In myriad ways, his story suggests he was coddled, although Peter Rodger defended his parenting in a statement after the murders:

> *I do mourn for the lonely boy Elliot was, who disappeared because of a monster of an illness in him that none of us knew was so severe. I wish I could turn the clock back. There are so many "If only's." I tried my best to do my duty as a father, but obviously my best was not enough . . . None of us understood what was in Elliot's head—he hid it from not only his family, but also from mental health professionals and law enforcement. Looking back now through a tragic hindsight, I have begun to understand that there are traits, markers if you will, that family members can look out for in loved ones.*

He and his ex-wife missed those traits and markers, which are apparent in the son's own words. His document suggests that Elliot complained incessantly about his inability to find a girlfriend. Perhaps it was a case of Aesop's The Boy Who Cried Wolf. When everything is "staggeringly horrific" to their prince-of-pain child, how do parents differentiate between a paper cut and a slashed throat? They become numbed to his tears. Elliot was a tireless umbrage-taker, toting forever a collection of any and all perceived affronts, however petty, including some dating to his early childhood. He was short of stature, and he never forgot a boyhood incident in which he was turned away from a carnival ride.

> *Being denied entry on a simple amusement park ride due to my height may seem like only a small injustice, but it was big for me at the time. Little did I know this injustice was very small indeed compared to all the things I'll be denied in the future because of my height.*

He returned to the issue of his height many times, including this note from fourth grade:

> *The first frustration of the year, which would remain for the rest of my life, was the fact that I was very short for my age . . . It instilled the first feelings of inferiority in me, and such feelings would only grow more volatile with time.*

His story is rife with self-absorption, as I have made clear, and he prattles on endlessly about his only two hobbies, skateboarding and the online video game World of Warcraft. Not surprisingly, he had few friends, and he reveals one cogent thought about his gaming hobby, where he played against unseen strangers on the Internet: "I hid myself away in the online World of Warcraft, a place where I felt comfortable and secure." Mostly, though, his stories reveal Rodger to be the spoiled, needy child that he was, including this pathetic anecdote about his need for validation from his brother Jazz, then a preschooler:

> In order to boost his high opinion of me, I often sugarcoated all of my early accomplishments, such as telling him that I was an expert skateboarder and video game player. People having a high opinion of me is what I've always wanted in life. It has always been of the utmost importance ... My little brother Jazz was the only one who had such an opinion, and that is why I enjoyed spending so much time with him, despite my envy of his social advantages.

Sense of Entitlement

Rodger's fathomless sense of entitlement leaps off nearly every page. At age nine, when his father bought a new home in high-toned Woodland Hills, he was devastated to learn that his new bedroom had neither a balcony nor a private bathroom. "I was furious, and I threw a huge crying tantrum," he wrote. Outdated computers were another endless cavil. At age 16, he wrote:

> My laptop was getting slower and slower. It wasn't a very powerful laptop, but it was the only computer I had

to play WoW [World of Warcraft] on. This was really
frustrating me, because eventually it became so slow
that it ruined my gaming experience. I kept pestering
my mother and father to get me a faster laptop that was
more efficient for gaming.

They gave in, as usual—salvaging his "gaming experience." After
Elliot finished high school, his mother—using the teen's hired
life coach Tony as her proxy—suggested that he find a job. You
will not be surprised to learn that the magnificent gentleman was
picky about suitable occupations:

I continued searching for a job, but I still wasn't able to
find one. I refused all of the jobs that Tony suggested
to me. The problem was that most of the jobs that were
available to me at the time were jobs I considered to be
beneath me. My mother wanted me to get a simple retail
job, and the thought of myself doing that was mortifying.
It would be completely against my character. I am an
intellectual who is destined for greatness. I would never
perform a low-class service job.

This was his experience when he finally agreed to work:

To my horror and humiliation, the job turned out to be a
menial custodial job, and I had to clean offices and even
the bathrooms. There was no way I would ever degrade
myself to such a level. I felt like utter shit from even

considering working at such a place. I only worked for a few hours while I thought about how to handle this foul situation . . . and on the next day I called to announce that I was quitting. That was the second and last "job" I would ever have. I only worked there for less than a day.

His parents were Rodger's sole source of support until the end, including college tuition, housing, food, clothing, his sweet BMW, and the $300 sunglasses he liked to brag about. Ostensibly, he attended college, but his autobiography suggests that he dropped nearly all of his classes every semester over conflicts with roommates or unresolved classmate crushes. This was his reaction to what seems like standard-issue college-guy hijinks, which Rodger had invited by revealing his virginity to roommates:

Every time they went out they kept yelling to me how they're going to sleep with hot girls that night. I knew they were just lying to make me jealous. They always made fun of me for being a virgin . . . I wanted to kill them both, but of course I was smart enough not to go through with that desire. All I could do was remember every single insult, so I can get revenge in a more efficient way in the future . . . When that time comes, I will crush all of my enemies in the most devastating and catastrophic way possible, and the results will be beautiful.

Money was another obsession, and he saw wealth as a solution to his pre-eminent problem. "If I become a multi-millionaire, I would be able to walk on the beach with a beautiful girlfriend, too, and my life would be complete," he wrote. "As I've always believed, I am destined for great things. Becoming a multi-millionaire at a young age is what I am meant for." But as he failed at both working and studying, it dawned on Rodger that he was not going to earn wealth legitimately. This prompted a crazed mission in the last year of his life to get rich quick by buying hundreds of lottery tickets, wasting thousands of his parents' dollars in a series of quixotic trips 300 miles (480 km) east to the Arizona border to buy into the big-money Powerball Lottery, which was not available in California. He was shocked when he didn't win:

> I sat very quiet and still in my desk chair for a long time, all of the emotion swept out of me. I didn't react with rage or anguish. I just sat there, cold and dead, mentally trying to contemplate what I had just done. I had driven all the way to Arizona just to buy lottery tickets, because I was so desperate for a happy life in which girls would be attracted to me; I was so certain I would win, building up all that hope, only to have it shattered right before me at just that moment.

He got in his car and drove to a park.

> Along the way, I saw couples strolling along the streets of Isla Vista, walking arm in arm; I saw groups of good-looking young people walking together, laughing and

enjoying each other's company. I felt completely dead inside, and torment racked my entire body, as I realized that I now had no chance to rise above them. I lost. When I got to the park I sat in my car for hours, crying and crying and crying. I wailed with agony. My tears streamed down my face and stained my collar. I couldn't take it anymore.

Triggered by Failure to Win Lottery

He telephoned his parents that day, and his brittle condition convinced them to make an appointment with a psychiatrist. As unlikely as it might seem, the lottery drawing in late 2012 was the final trigger that nudged Rodger toward his deadly rampage 18 months later. He wrote: "I realized that I had to start planning and preparing for the Day of Retribution."

His first step was to get a pistol, which seemed to transform wee, mousy Elliot into a Chad Thundercock. He paid for the gun, a Glock 34 semi-automatic, then took possession in mid-December after California's mandatory waiting period expired. He wrote: "After I picked up the handgun, I brought it back to my room and felt a new sense of power. I was now armed. Who's the alpha male now, bitches?"

The final 10,000 words of his autobiography amount to a frightening checkerboard of planning notes and macho snarls. For example, he spun a misogynist theorem about the failings of uncontrolled breeding that would make Margaret Atwood shiver:

I concluded that women are flawed . . . They are like animals, completely controlled by their primal, depraved emotions and impulses. That is why they are attracted to barbaric, wild, beast-like men. They are beasts themselves . . . Women should not have the right to choose who to mate with. That choice should be made for them by civilized men of intelligence. If women had the freedom to choose which men to mate with, like they do today, they would breed with stupid, degenerate men, which would only produce stupid, degenerate offspring. This in turn would hinder the advancement of humanity . . . Women are like a plague that must be quarantined . . . I am one of the few people on this world who has the intelligence to see this. I am like a god . . .

Tell-Tale Videos Ignored

As with many mass shooters, Rodger dropped hints at his plan that should have led to intervention. He uploaded three YouTube videos with troubling messages, one of them a full five weeks before his rampage. He ended one:

I desire girls. I'm sexually attracted to girls. But girls are not sexually attracted to me. And there's a major problem with that, a major problem. That's a problem that I intend to rectify. I, in all my magnificence and power, I will not let this fly. It's an injustice that needs to be dealt with.

His mother saw the video and called the police, which was both a bold step and a form of outsourcing her concerns. Rodger recounted what happened:

> *I heard a knock on my apartment door. I opened it to see about seven police officers asking for me. As soon as I saw those cops, the biggest fear I had ever felt in my life overcame me . . . Apparently, someone saw my videos and became instantly suspicious of me. They called some sort of health agency, who called the police to check up on me . . . The police interrogated me outside for a few minutes, asking me if I had suicidal thoughts. I tactfully told them that it was all a misunderstanding, and they finally left. If they had demanded to search my room . . . that would have ended everything. For a few horrible seconds I thought it was all over. When they left, the biggest wave of relief swept over me.*

Once again, someone—both the police and his parents, in this case—had failed when given a heads-up that could have headed off mass murder. By the time Rodger reloaded those videos and one other on his Day of Retribution, Saturday, May 23, 2014, it was too late. Here is an excerpt from his vile final video:

> *I take great pleasure in slaughtering all of you. You will finally see that I am, in truth, the superior one, the true alpha male. Yes, after I have annihilated every single girl in the sorority house, I'll take to the streets of Isla Vista*

and slay every single person I see there . . . I will be a
god compared to you, you will all be animals, you are
animals and I will slaughter you like animals. . . . I
waited a long time for this. I'll give you exactly what you
deserve, all of you. All you girls who rejected me, looked
down upon me, you know, treated me like scum while
you gave yourselves to other men. And all of you men
for living a better life than me, all of you sexually active
men. I hate you. I hate all of you. I can't wait to give you
exactly what you deserve, annihilation.

Claimed Victimhood

Rodger wrote and edited his autobiography until his final hours.
In the concluding paragraph, he donned the cloak of victimhood
one final time:

> *I am the true victim in all of this. I am the good guy.*
> *Humanity struck at me first by condemning me to*
> *experience so much suffering. I didn't ask for this. I*
> *didn't want this. I didn't start this war . . . But I will finish*
> *it by striking back. I will punish everyone. And it will be*
> *beautiful. Finally, at long last, I can show the world my*
> *true worth.*

If Rodger was a victim in any sense, he was a victim of his own
damaged masculinity and virulent misogyny, compounded by
parental myopia or slacking. This man-child shot himself in the

Happy memories of Elliot Rodger's victim, Christopher Michaels-Martinez, outside the entrance to IV Deli Mart at Isla Vista, California. The UCSB student was gunned down and killed in Rodger's pointless rampage.

head 22 years and ten months after his arrival at that London hospital in 1991. He did not die heroically as an alpha male, but as a broken boy, a mouse who chose the easy way out of life. Jessica Valenti, an American feminist author and journalist, says the criminal madness of men like Rodger and Pittsburgh's Sodini is a herald of the country's cultural failings. Writing in *The New York Times* she said:

> *Part of the problem is that American culture still largely sees men's sexism as something innate rather*

than deviant. And in a world where sexism is deemed natural, the misogynist tendencies of mass shooters become afterthoughts rather than predictable and stark warnings. The truth is that in addition to not protecting women, we are failing boys: failing to raise them to believe they can be men without inflicting pain on others, failing to teach them that they are not entitled to women's sexual attention, and failing to allow them an outlet for understandable human fear and foibles that will not label them "weak" or unworthy. Not every attack is preventable, but the misogyny that drives them is.

Chapter 6.
Journal of a
Broken Mind

Mass killers do not come with a centaur's horns or a swastika carved into their forehead, à la Charles Manson. Most of them look like the rest of us—average Joes. Stephen Paddock, who set a record by killing 58 people in Las Vegas on October 1, 2017, raining down more than a thousand shots from his hotel room window onto a crowded outdoor music festival, was a 64-year-old Baby Boomer who looked like a TV sitcom disheveled uncle straight from Central Casting.

A retired accountant and successful real estate investor, Paddock did not leave a suicide note or a manifesto before he died, unlike most other shooters. The Clark County sheriff revealed that Paddock was a high-stakes gambler who was on a losing streak and doctors said he was possibly bipolar. Also, some witnesses have said that they heard him expressing conspiratorial anti-government beliefs typical of the right wing. But these factors alone don't necessarily make a mass murderer. Paddock didn't suddenly crack that day either, because the evidence shows that he carefully prepared his attack over a number of weeks. His father wasn't the greatest role model. Benjamin Hoskins Paddock was a notorious bank robber who was featured on the FBI most wanted list in 1969, and was described by the bureau as "psychopathic with suicidal tendencies," "armed and very dangerous." But the indications are that Stephen didn't grow up under the influence of his absentee father. So the mystery of why Paddock fired on the crowd of festival-goers will perhaps never be solved.

Devin Kelley, who killed 26 people just five weeks later at a country church near San Antonio, Texas, was a chubby, baby-faced everyman, albeit with a bad beard. A lost motorist would have felt no qualms about asking directions from Paddock, Kelley, or another seemingly benign man who emerged as a mass killer: James Holmes. But unlike Paddock, or Kelley for that matter, Holmes left behind him a wealth of materials, more than most attackers, for the world to ponder.

Bright Kid

James Holmes grew up in California in a traditional nuclear family—mom, dad, and two kids, each of them an introvert. His parents, Bob and Arlene, were practicing Lutherans who identified as prayerful conservative Christians. Bob was a statistician, and Arlene a nurse. Though shy and socially awkward, James was a bright kid and a good student.

"He seemed happy enough, just pretty much a normal everyday kid growing up," Bob Holmes told the BBC in 2017. He was the antithesis of a problem child.

"In retrospect," his mother said, "I think he was too good. Maybe I should have worried about the fact he was so good, but as a mother you can worry about just about anything."

In fact, his parents missed indicators of trouble suppressed below their son's obedient veneer. When depression set in during James's adolescence his mother dismissed it as typical teen irritability, even though he tried to leave clues about his despair. In his journal, he revealed that he cut a wrist in an act of "parasuicide"—a non-lethal suicidal gesture. His mother noticed the wound, which Holmes dismissed as a paper cut, but she naively bought his explanation. Obliquely recounting

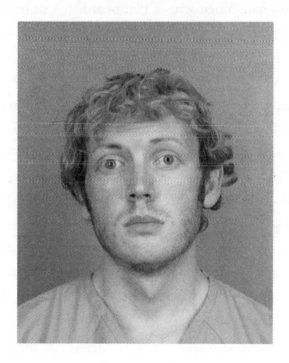

Beneath the veneer of obedience, James Holmes was slowly falling apart. His parents failed to spot the early indicators of a deeply troubled mind.

the incident in his journal, he wrote: "No further investigation. Clean bill of health. Decided to dedicate life to killing others so that I could live." He was 11 years old at the time. Thirteen years later, in 2012, Holmes acted on that vow when he attacked an Aurora, Colorado, movie theater.

After wading through the written and recorded thoughts of many dozens of mass killers from around the world, I concluded that the record accumulated by James Holmes stands out in several ways. First, he was the rare contemporary U.S. mass killer who survived his attack. Out of the 27 U.S. mass shootings since 1949 that have had nine or more fatalities, Holmes is one of just seven perpetrators who survived. The perpetrator in each of the nation's eight most deadly mass shootings was killed by his own hand, by law enforcers, or by civilians who interceded. Second, the well of materials from and about Holmes is deeper than most: eerie text messages he sent to love interests that augured trouble ahead; creepy videotapes of his interview with detectives after the murders, in which he used bags placed over his hands (to preserve forensic evidence) as puppets talking to one another; analyses by psychiatrists who treated or examined Holmes before and after his attack.

Most importantly, his criminal trial evidence included his extraordinary journal, which he entitled "Insights into the Mind of Madness." A number of media stories about Holmes have characterized his journal as a rant. It is not. Many of the written leavings of killers come across as screeds or self-obsessed jeremiads because so many of them blame anyone but themselves. By contrast, Holmes's complaints were largely

Scene of carnage: The Century 16 movie theater in Aurora.

focused inward. His battle was internal, not against the imagined human enemies that so many killers choose—women, minorities, happy people—and his journal was a self-examination of his own failings and the encroachment of homicidal psychosis. Those 30 pages, handwritten in loopy, tremulous script in a grid-lined school computation notebook, reveal the evolutionary process as Holmes went from pondering *whether* to kill to making detailed plans on how best to kill as many victims as possible. Ultimately, he concluded that he had no choice but to "embrace [my] longstanding hatred of mankind."

Failed Relationship

After finishing high school in San Diego in 2006, Holmes earned an undergraduate degree in neuroscience after four years at the University of California, Riverside. His grade point average was nearly perfect—3.949 on a 4.0 scale. He had planned to go on to earn a Ph.D. in neuroscience, motivated in part by a yearning to understand his own disturbed mind, but he was disappointed when six prestigious universities turned him down. As a result, he withdrew to his bedroom in a funk for months. At his mother's insistence, Holmes then applied to second-tier doctoral programs, and he was accepted at the University of Colorado's medical campus in Aurora, in metropolitan Denver. Supported by a federal grant and a university stipend totaling nearly $30,000, Holmes moved from San Diego into a graduate student apartment at 1690 Paris Street, adjacent to the campus.

He seemed to have found his tribe as he began his studies in June 2011. His classes were full of fellow budding scientists who tended to be nerdy and socially awkward, just like him. That fall, Holmes began a romance with a classmate, a south Asian woman named Gargi Datta. She was his first girlfriend, at age 23. Datta later described Holmes as smart, polite, and shy, but she said he was more invested in the relationship than she was. She ended things in February 2012. It was a cordial breakup, and they maintained contact, but Holmes later told a shrink that depression related to the failed relationship was a catalyst for a psychotic decline that culminated in the movie theater attack five months later. "My mind was kind of falling apart," he told Dr. William Reid after the murders.

Reveals Homicidal Thoughts

While talking with Datta, Holmes began revealing for the first time the homicidal thoughts that had infested his mind since adolescence. At Datta's suggestion, Holmes sought counseling at the university health center and on March 21, 2012, he began a series of visits with a campus psychiatrist, Dr. Lynne Fenton. During their first session she prescribed a 50-milligram dose of the anti-depressant Zoloft. Holmes documented the effect of the drug in his journal: "First appearance of mania occurs, not good mania. Anxiety and fear disappears. No more fear, no more fear of failure. Fear of failure drove determination to improve, better and succeed in life. No fear of consequences." A few days after he began taking Zoloft, Holmes had a text exchange with his ex-girlfriend:

> *Holmes: what I feel like doing is evil so can't do that*
>
> *Datta: what is so evil that you want to do?*
>
> *Holmes: Kill people of course*
>
> *Datta: What would taking a life give you?*
>
> *Holmes: Human capital. Some people may make 1 million dollars, others 100,000. But life is priceless. You take away life and your human capital is limitless*
>
> *Datta: What would you do with the human capital?*
>
> *Holmes: Have a more meaningful life.*

Datta later said that she thought Holmes was joking. He wasn't. He acknowledged during subsequent appointments with Dr. Fenton that homicidal thoughts were occurring three or four times a day. She then upped his Zoloft dosage to 100 milligrams. Fenton's concern grew with each session with Holmes, and after his fourth appointment, on April 17, Fenton wrote in her case notes: "Psychotic level thinking . . . Guarded, paranoid, hostile thoughts he won't elaborate on."

Deepening Psychosis

By that point, ten months into his doctoral studies, Holmes had resolved to withdraw from the program. The last straw was his failure in an important oral presentation at semester's end. He shared the news with Fenton in their final visit. She was so disturbed by Holmes's mental state that she contacted the campus police to ask whether he was permitted to own weapons, and she also took the unusual step of calling his parents. Arlene Holmes once again underestimated her son's dire mental state. She recounted the Fenton conversation in a BCC interview.

"She said, 'Do you know that he is not going to continue in school?' I thought that was the purpose of her phone call, and I said, 'Did he ask you to call me?' And she said, 'No he didn't want me to call you, and he didn't want you to worry.' I was reassured by her phone call, rather than alarmed."

Amid his deepening psychosis that spring, James Holmes engaged in a flirtatious relationship with another classmate, Hillary Allen. They went hiking together once, saw one another regularly in class, and occasionally exchanged texts. Holmes clearly was interested in her, but she wasn't into him—making it clear, for example, that he should not interpret their hike as a date. She was a casual friend who admired Holmes's intellect, and she was concerned after learning that he was planning to leave school. At 10:30 p.m. on July 8, 12 days before the theater attack, the two had a text exchange:

> *Holmes: Have yuh ever met someone with dysphoric mania?*
> *Allen: No. What is that?*
> *Holmes: It's what I've got. Always it's in your best interest to avoid me, am bad news bears.*
> *Allen: I just looked it up. Is it manageable? I've struggled with depression too (comes from other stuff) it's hard to deal with*
> *Holmes: It was, floodgates open now.*

Like a good friend, Allen asked at the end of that exchange: "Are you ok?" Holmes replied, "Yep." But, of course, he wasn't.

Weapons Arsenal

Two months earlier, Holmes had begun assembling an arsenal and head-to-toe tactical gear in his grad student apartment, according to receipts later cataloged by detectives. His first purchase, on May 18, was a $120 gas mask, the SGE 150, which he ordered online. Over the ensuing three weeks, he then spent more than $2,000 to purchase a Glock pistol, a Smith & Wesson assault rifle, a Remington shotgun, several laser sights, holsters, and extra cartridge magazines at various outdoors retailers, including Gander Mountain, Bass Pro Shops, and Sportsman's Guide.

With no criminal record, Holmes breezed through the federal firearms approval process. He used PayPal to buy $900 worth of body armor to protect his torso, arms, and groin and spent $337 on a U.S. Army-style combat helmet. On top of that, he also bought a military assault vest, boots, two tear gas grenades, a knife, handcuffs, membership to a shooting range, dozens of targets, and more than 6,000 rounds of ammunition.

Journal of a Killer

Concurrent with this shopping spree, Holmes sat in the isolation of his apartment and created an extraordinary record of the psychology of a mass killer, as he transitioned from whether and why to how and when. The first 15 pages of his journal are taken up with contemplations of existential questions about life and death. He concludes that section by veering off into a metaphysical rumination about our relationship with the broader universe. Arriving at no satisfactory answer, he distills his musings into a single question—"*Why?*"—which he pleadingly, metronomically repeats nearly 300 times, filling eight full pages of the booklet, each page in larger script than the last. The final page in that series contains one last outsized copy of the question Why? The final eight pages of the journal turn from philosophy to the logistics of mass murder.

He dedicated the first full page of "Insights into the Mind of Madness" to this note:

The Questions
What is the meaning of life?
What is the meaning of death?

Other excerpts from the first 15 pages:

*Can a person have both no value AND be ultimately good AND/OR ultimately evil in value? *unknown . . .*

Violence is a false response to truth while giving the illusion of truth. This is widely understood with murder being unjust.

However, mankind hasn't found a better alternative & there is still mass violence, war, and unfortunately those forms of violence are misleadingly still justified . . .

Alternatives to death:

1. *Ignore the problem.*
   If the problem or question doesn't exist, then the solution is irrelevant.
   Didn't work. Forms of escapism tried included reading, television, and alcohol.

2. *Delay the problem.*
   Live in the moment without concern for answering the problem at present.
   Didn't work. Pursued knowledge to increase the capacity for answering the questions with improved cognitive function.

3. *Pawn the problem.*

If one can't answer the question themselves,
get someone else to answer it.
Didn't work. Everyone else didn't know the
solution either.

4. *Love.*
    Hate.
    Despite knowing death is false and a
    suboptimal response, I couldn't find a working
    alternative . . .

Self-Diagnosis of Symptoms

On subsequent pages, Holmes focuses on a subsection he entitled "Self-Diagnosis of Broken Mind." His self-described roster of personal maladies comprised: dysphoric mania; generalized anxiety disorder/social anxiety disorder/OCD/PTSD (chronic); Asperger's syndrome/autism; ADHD; schizophrenia; body dysmorphic disorder; borderline narcissistic, anxious, avoidant, and obsessive-compulsive personality disorder; chronic insomnia; psychosis; trichotillomania [compulsive hair-pulling]; adjustment disorder; pain disorder; and restless leg syndrome.

He also lists detailed descriptions of the symptoms of these disorders, including catatonia, fatigue, an inability to communicate, and obsessive behavior often focused on certain body parts, including his hair, nose, ears, teeth, and penis, the latter of which he feared was scarred or disfigured from "excessive stimulation," undefined "accidents" as a child, and an allergic reaction to soap. He cites this final symptom: "The obsession to kill since I was a kid, [which] with age became more and more realistic." Holmes explained that his early fantasies about murder focused on destroying the world with nuclear bombs or biological agents. He then considered but rejected serial murder. He continued:

> And finally, the last escape, mass murder at the movies. Obsession onset > 10 years ago. So anyways, that's my mind. It is broken. I tried to fix it. I made it my sole conviction but using something that's broken to fix itself proved insurmountable . . . Despite my biological shortcomings I have fought and fought. Always defending against predetermination and the fallibility of man. There is one more battle to fight with life. To face death, embrace the longstanding hatred of mankind and overcome all fear in certain death.

Holmes followed that with a brief poem he entitled "Futility":

> The mind is a prison of uncertainty.
> Trillions of cells guard it for eternity.
> O' where art though [sic] master key?
> Destroy the mind and be free.

Planning the Attack

After the many pages of "Why?" Holmes dedicates the final quarter of the journal to the planning of his attack, including four pages with detailed diagrams of his target, the Century 16 movie theater, adjacent to a shopping mall on East Alameda Avenue in Aurora, four miles from the killer's apartment. His planning notes reveal that he rejected bombs ("too regulated and suspicious"); biological warfare ("too impatient. Requires extensive knowledge, chemistry equipment"); and serial murder ("too personal, too much evidence, easily caught, few kills"). He mulled an airport as a target but rejected the idea because he feared it would mark him as a "terrorist." He makes an important point about his motive—or "message"—in the entry rejecting airports as a venue:

> Terrorism isn't the message. The message is there is no message. Most fools will misinterpret correlation for causation, namely relationship and work failure as causes. Both were expediting catalysts, not the reason. The causation being my state of mind for the past 15 years.

Thus, he settled on movie theater mass murder, listing these pros: "Maximum casualties, easily performed w/firearms although primitive in nature. No fear of consequences, being caught 99% certain." About his random victims, he notes: "The cruel twists of fate are unkind to the misfortunate." He closes his journal with this note: "The reason why life should exist is as arbitrary as the reason why it shouldn't. Life shouldn't exist."

Holmes was a busy fellow in the final hours before the assault. He completed the bomb-boobytrapping of his apartment, hoping to blow up law enforcers who came after his attack, then he mailed his journal to Dr. Fenton. And he may have had a last-minute attack of conscience: He dialed a mental health hotline, but the call disconnected after nine seconds.

Movie Theater Carnage

The shooter bought a ticket online for the July 20 midnight showing at Century 16 of the newly released "Batman" sequel, *The Dark Night Rises*. Wearing inconspicuous clothing but with his hair dyed shocking orange, he arrived early and passed through the lobby and into theater No. 9. He then left through an emergency exit door, which he propped open, and went to his car to don his assault gear and retrieve his weapons. When he returned to No. 9 via the emergency exit at 12:10 a.m., five minutes after the movie began, he was dressed to kill. The auditorium was from the American multiplex template, with seating for roughly 350 people in about 20 steeply sloped rows.

As he had planned, Holmes moved to a position at the bottom of the packed auditorium, just in front of the screen. He must have seemed like a specter to the crowd, with four guns dangling, the gas mask, body armor, and a fringe of orange hair peeking out from beneath his combat helmet. First of all, he tossed his two tear gas grenades, then he began firing at his "misfortunate" targets. As with many mass shootings, it took a few moments for those in the theater to comprehend what was happening—that it wasn't part of the entertainment. Many fled toward the exits, and others dove to the floor. Luck saved some; fateful bullets found others. In a matter of minutes James Holmes ended 12 lives and wounded some 70 other moviegoers. Among

Boarded up: Holmes's apartment was booby-trapped from end to end. A deadly mixture of bullets, gunpowder and flammable liquid was set to explode.

the dead was a six-year-old girl, Veronica Moser-Sullivan, who had gone to see the movie with her mother. The killer had finally fully embraced his simmering hatred.

Holmes had expected to die, so he must have been surprised when he was arrested outside the theater, as though he were a common thief instead of a mass killer. Newspapers around the world published his crazed mugshot, with the orange hair and bug eyes. He was charged with murder, of course, and after nearly three years of pretrial parrying among prosecutors, defense attorneys, and psychiatrists, he faced a jury in 2015.

The panel of 12 peers listened to three months of testimony and arguments, then rejected his insanity defense and convicted Holmes of murder. Eleven jurors voted in favor of capital punishment, but a lack of unanimity saved his life when a single juror refused to go along. Instead, the jury recommended a sentence of life in prison without the possibility of parole. In the unconstrained American manner of sentencing, he was sent away for 12 life sentences plus an additional 3,318 years. (Compare that with Scandinavian justice: Anders Breivik, who killed 77 people in Norway in 2011, got his nation's maximum sentence: 21 years.)

Why Did it Happen?

Amateurs and professionals alike have pondered the broken mind and twisted reasoning of Holmes since the night of his attack. As Dr. Dale Archer wrote in his blog: "One thing is clear: it is possible to be very intelligent and still suffer from serious mental illness." The killer's mother, Arlene, said:

> If you had told me this would happen to us, I just wouldn't have believed it. Not in your wildest dreams would you think your son would shoot strangers. For someone who loved kids and dogs and always did his homework and his chores. You can't believe it is possible for anyone to cause that much harm, let alone the man you raised.

At his trial, prosecutor George Brauchler offered an oversimplified analysis of what went wrong in Holmes's life.

> *He's not going to get that PhD. He's not going to find that*
> *woman to love and have that house with those two kids*
> *and the dog. And that's when he turns his sights on this*
> *lifelong passion that he's had to kill other people, and*
> *that's when we see him start to set these things in motion.*

Dr. William Reid, the forensic psychiatrist who examined Holmes after the murders, probably got closer to the truth when he said that Holmes had a lifelong "aversion to mankind." And the BBC certainly got it right when it declared the case "another tragic collision of mental breakdown with America's lax gun laws."

By the date of that dreadful night in the theater, after 13 years of hiding his sickness from his family, Holmes was consumed by his alienation and bottomless despair. It seems clear that his actions were a form of suicide by proxy, even though he survived. By ending all those lives, James Holmes knew he was destroying his own.

Chapter 7.
Murder in Black and White

Marsha Spencer had hoped to find a window into Dylann Roof's soul when she got a chance to face him in court on the day he was condemned to die, January 11, 2017. Spencer was a member of Mother Emanuel AME, the historic black church in Charleston, South Carolina, where Roof had slaughtered the beloved senior pastor and eight members 19 months earlier.

"Who are you?" Spencer demanded of Roof. "What happened to you, Dylann?"

Sitting as inert as a Confederate statue, Roof did not budge. He would not oblige Spencer—or any of the other family and friends of the victims who spoke that day—with so much as a nonverbal acknowledgement. His eyes were downcast, his soul barricaded.

"How dare you sit here every day looking dumb-faced, and acting like you did nothing wrong," said Ashland Temoney, whose aunt was one of his victims.

"I wish you would look at me, boy," said Jamie Scott, who lost a nephew, "but I know that you can hear me!" Hear, yes. But comprehend? That is an open question for all who have tried to understand how an Internet-inspired South Carolinian with a ninth-grade education convinced himself to march off to a one-man race war against a Bible study group.

A blank-faced Dylann Roof is taken away under armed guard.

Victims Shot While Praying

On June 17, 2015, Roof raced 100 miles (160 km) in his black Hyundai sedan from his trailer park home in central South Carolina to coastal Charleston. He drove through the city to the tourist district, where Mother Emanuel sits like a glistening white opal on Calhoun Street, a few blocks from a harbor famously guarded by Fort Sumter. Roof devilishly chose that church because it is iconic as one of the first independent black houses of worship in the U.S. Founded more than two centuries ago, Mother Emanuel is a mecca for godly African Americans. Roof had carefully cased the venue during reconnaissance trips, and his target was a Bible meeting held each Wednesday evening at eight in the basement fellowship hall.

Arriving 17 minutes late and entering through a basement door, the skinny blond Caucasian might have seemed like a wraith to the 12 black men and women gathered around their Bibles. A black tactical bag—like a gigantic fanny pack—covered his crotch halfway to his knees, and concealed inside was a .45-caliber Glock handgun and 88 rounds of ammunition. He paused at the church door to adjust the absurdly oversized bag, and later said he was certain that someone would recognize it as a gun holster. But no one did, and he was greeted as a friend, not the enemy he was. Senior Pastor Clementa Pinckney, a long-serving South Carolina state senator, fetched a chair for the stranger. He sat down with the group and for 45 minutes joined in their scriptural analysis, several times quibbling with them.

At 9:05 p.m., as the 12 nodded their heads in an eyes-closed prayer, Roof extracted his weapon and then stood up and began firing, targeting Pastor Pinckney with the first three shots. For six terrifying minutes, Roof moved from one man and woman to the next, squeezing off multiple shots at close range against each defenseless target. He paused five times to reload, snapping in extra magazine clips filled with punishing hollow-point bullets, which mushroom when they contact human tissue.

In the midst of the murders, a young man in the group, Tywanza Sanders, tried to reason with Roof. In essence, he said you don't have to do this. The killer replied: "I have to do this because you are raping our women and taking over the world." He then pumped five shots into Sanders, who at age 26 was the youngest of the nine victims. (The oldest was Susie Jackson, 87. Roof shot her 11 times.) Three people cheated death, including Tywanza's mother, Felicia Sanders, and her five-year-old granddaughter. Roof also spared Polly Shepherd, a 72-year-old retired nurse, as a designated witness. "We need someone to survive," Roof told her, "because I'm gonna shoot myself, and you'll be the only survivor." She was calling the police on her cellphone as Roof left the church.

He did not work up the nerve for suicide and was arrested 16 hours later in Shelby, North Carolina, 250 miles (400 km) north of Charleston. FBI agents were soon asking him the same question that Marsha Spencer would later pose: Why?

White Supremacist

"I had to do it because somebody had to do something," Roof told the agents. "Black people are killing white people every day on the street, and they are raping white women. What I did is so minuscule to what they're doing to white people every day all the time."

He framed his crime as "political" and proudly acknowledged that he was a white supremacist.

"Our people are superior," declared the 22-year-old. "That's just the fact."

He was a shoddy specimen of white superiority. Roof grew up poor in a fractured family; his parents were finished with one another by the time he arrived in the world. His mother gave him his fancy name—Dylann Storm Roof—because it reminded her of one of those urbane characters in a television soap opera. He attended public schools that were predominantly black, which is typical of the bifurcated education system in the American South, where parents of means pay tuition to send their children to private schools, and his schooling ended prematurely during his first year of high school.

Roof is often described as a "lone wolf," the global label used for terrorists who "self-radicalize" without guidance or assistance from others, often influenced by content they dredge up on the Internet. But his crimes had many antecedents, certainly including the thousands of southern lynchings during the Jim Crow era. He belongs to a brotherhood of contemporary racist killers.

Other Racist Killers

Two years before he massacred 17 people in February 2018 at his former Parkland, Florida, high school, confessed gunman

Nikolas Cruz carried a book bag inscribed "I hate niggers," a message he bluntly repeated in 2016 to a caseworker from the Florida Department of Children and Families. He expanded his roster of hate to included "jews, niggers, immigrants" in an Instagram group he founded.

Columbine's Eric Harris frequently ranted racial hatred, including an entry from his journal that cast a broad net of bigotry: "And I am one racist motherfucker too, fuck the niggers and spics and chinks, unless they are cool, but sometimes they are so fucking retarded they deserve to be ripped on." Karl Pierson, who killed a teacher during a shooting rampage in 2013 at his own Colorado high school, often used racist language too, including a throwback message written on his school planner: "Jim Crow was mah nigga."

JEFF WEISE

In 2004, a bright but disaffected Native American teenager stumbled onto an Internet forum occupied by neo-Nazis. In his first post, he naively (or honestly) offered a full identification:

> *Hello all. My name is Jeff Weise, a Native American from the Red Lake "Indian" reservation in Minnesota. I'm interested in joining the group, as I support your ideals, and even though I am young I still want to join. What is the age requirement (if any)?*

He quickly got a reply from a suspicious member. Weise, 15 years old, wrote back:

What brings me to the forum? Well, I stumbled across the site in my study of the Third Reich as well as Nazism, amongst other things. I guess I've always carried a natural admiration for Hitler and his ideals, and his courage to take on larger nations . . .

When I was growing up, I was taught (like others) that Nazis were (are) evil and that Hitler was a very evil man etc . . . Upon reading up on his actions, the ideals and issues the German Third Reich addressed, I began to see how much of a lie had been painted about them . . .

It kind of angers me how people pass pre-judgement on someone if they even so much as say something like "I support what Hitler did," without even hearing what you have to say. This goes double if you're ethnic . . . It's easy to see that even today people are trying to destroy the image of a man who deserves great respect . . .

One year and two days after he wrote those words, Weise went on a rampage in Red Lake, killing his grandfather and the man's companion, then slaughtering seven people at his school before committing suicide. (There was no apparent racist component to the shootings; all victims were Natives. He was depressed, on Prozac, and complained of teasing, but no clear-cut motive materialized.)

Among the growing club of mass killers, Weise was not alone in his admiration for the Nazis and Hitler. The Columbine killers launched their attack on April 20 because it was Hitler's birthday. A Nazi salute and an enthusiastic "Sieg Heil!" are de rigueur on mass shooters' videos. More than a dozen from this club have commented favorably on Hitler, including Columbine's Harris, Canada's Marc Lépine and Kimveer Gill, Finland's Pekka-Eric Auvinen, Arizona's Jared Loughner, and the romantically challenged killers Elliot Rodger of California and Chris Harper-Mercer of Oregon.

Their fascination with the Third Reich is understandable. Many of these killers have left records spelling out their fantasies of causing widespread, or even global destruction. So Hitler, one of history's more accomplished mass killers, was an apt role model. For the Americans in this club, the admiration was mutual. Hitler's notion of Aryan superiority was inspired in part by the low regard for slaves and, later, freed black citizens, in the U.S. Like Colorado's Pierson, he thought Jim Crow laws were a splendid idea, and he used them against Jews and other targeted ethnicities. Inspired by their German ideological progenitors, the fundamental underpinning of neo-Nazis is an obsession with eugenics and miscegenation, even if they don't understand the words.

And that points back to an anecdote concerning Minnesota's Jeffrey Weise. He began using the handle NativeNazi on the online forum, though the racial dynamics with his white nationalist forum-mates grew rather mottled. Weise argued in favor of racial purity—for his tribe, not necessarily whites—and he was clearly thrilled that someone was interested in his thoughts, even though many of the forum-users' questions tried to draw out racist responses from the teen. One contributor asked, " . . . in what way(s) do you feel Jewish power has affected the lives of Native Americans in general?" Weise replied:

> *If I asked your average teenager on this reservation: "Are you proud to be Native?" the answer I would get is, "hell yeah dawg." . . . Most of the Natives I know have been poisoned by what they were taught in school. The basic "Nazi=Bad, Jew=Good. Defend Jew at all costs." You get the idea. The public school system has done more harm than good, and as a result it has left many on this reservation misled and misinformed . . . What ways has the Jewish power affected us in general? Ever since the Jewish post-war propaganda has been taught in our school systems (on reservations), a lot have been brainwashed into thinking purity is wrong, at least that's my take on it. I can't help but notice how many pure-blooded Natives there are left . . .*

In answer to another question, Weise hinted at the violence to come—then added a plaintive postscript that began with a showcase of his wasted wit:

> *I wear combat boots (with my pant legs tucked into them), wear a trench coat, and at the last basketball game my friend Mac (who happens to wear a black trench coat like mine), did a Sieg Heil during the national anthem (for shock value), so they had us pegged as "Trench Coat Mafia." My "friend" Rose even said that I fit the profile*

of a school shooter that she saw on 60 Minutes. They
also pinned it on me because 4/20 happens to be Adolf
Hitler's birthday, and I seem to be the only one who
promotes National Socialist beliefs (not the stereotypical
"White Power" bs you hear racists shouting, either). So
it's not hard to label a school shooter . . .

      PS: I'm not a white supremacist; can't even spell
it. I'm a Native American, Ojibwa, living on the Redlake
Indian Reservation in Minnesota, and let's not turn this
into a hardcore political discussion about my political
ideals, ok?

JIM DAVID ADKISSON

Four years after Weise's puzzling spree, Jim David Adkisson emerged as a prototype for the newly emboldened class of racist white men in America. On July 27, 2008, Adkisson, a 58-year-old unemployed truck driver, stalked into a packed Unitarian Universalist church in Knoxville, Tennessee, as children were performing the musical *Annie.* He then pulled a sawed-off Remington shotgun from his guitar case and fired three blasts of birdshot before he was quickly subdued. Two people were killed and six were injured. The dead included Greg McKendry, 60, who stepped in front of the barrel to save others.

    The church heroes minimized Adkisson's headline ignominy when they promptly wrestled him down, so the shooting did not attract much attention beyond Tennessee and the UU church world. But it was a forerunner of violence by

Killer Jim Adkisson told detectives: "See, if you'd met me in a bar [or] on a street, you'd say, 'Well, that's a nice fella,' and I am."

rabid right-wingers focused on race or minority faiths: six people were killed by a white supremacist in 2012 at a Sikh temple near Milwaukee, Wisconsin; three lost their lives at the hands of an aged neo-Nazi in 2014, at a Jewish facility in the Kansas City suburb of Overland Park; and then came Roof in 2015.

Adkisson lugged a heavy bag of bigotry, which he delineated in the 1,000-word disquisition on race, sexuality, and politics he wrote before the shooting. He grew up west of Knoxville and did an Army hitch as a mechanic in the 1970s. However, on account of a drinking problem and moodiness, he couldn't keep a job or sustain a relationship when he got home from the service. His fifth wife, Liza Alexander, left him in 2000 after he threatened murder–suicide. Like Dylann Roof, Adkisson wasn't much of a role model for upright neo-Nazis, because by 2008 he was terminally unemployed and surviving on welfare and food stamps. Yet in the twilight of a two-term Republican presidency, the resident of a Republican-dominated state managed to blame liberal Democrats for his failures. Friends and neighbors said he extracted talking points from blustery books by conservative Fox News luminaries like Bill O'Reilly, Sean Hannity, and Bernard Goldberg.

"This was a hate crime," Adkisson wrote. "I hate the damned left-wing liberals . . . These liberals are working together to attack every decent and honorable institution in our nation. They are trying to turn this country into a communist state. Shame on them." He chose the liberal Knoxville UU church because his ex-wife Alexander once was a member there. "The Unitarian Universalist Church is not a church. It is a cult," he wrote. "This is a collection of sick, weird, and homosexual people . . . They embrace every pervert that comes down the pike." He continued:

> They call themselves "progressive." How is a white woman having a nigger baby progress? How is a man sticking his dick up another man's ass progress? It is

an abomination before the Lord. It takes warped minds to hate America like they do. It makes me so angry! I cannot live with it anymore! The environmental nuts have to be stopped too!

Just as Roof and so many others among the new breed of spree killers would do, Adkisson imagined that he was part of a tribe—that he was going to "kickstart a revolution," in Eric Harris's infamous phrase. "I would like to encourage other like-minded people to do as I have done," Adkisson wrote. "If life is no longer worth living, do not just kill yourself. Do something worthwhile for your country before you go. Kill liberals."

The June 2008 primary election victories that cinched Barack Obama's Democratic presidential nomination served as a trigger for his violence.

I am protesting against the Democratic National Convention for running a radical, leftist candidate for president of the United States, namely Osama Hussein Obama (Yo Mama!!!). He has no experience. He has no brains. He is a joke. He is dangerous to America. Hell! He even looks like Curious George!

He went on to rant about the media ("the propaganda wing of the Democratic Party"), and he blamed the Democrats for bringing ruination to the military, religion, education, the U.S. Supreme Court, the battle against terrorism—even the Boy Scouts.

I wanted to kill every Democrat in the U.S. Senate, every Democrat in the U.S. House of Representatives, and all 100 people in Bernard Goldberg's book entitled 100 People Who Are Screwing Up America. I would like to kill everyone in the mainstream news media.

He said he settled instead for the UU "foot soldiers."

His bloodbath against unarmed, peace-loving innocents left Adkisson feeling pleased with himself. "See, if you'd met me in a bar [or] on a street, you'd say, 'Well, that's a nice fella,'" he told detectives. "And I am."

Like Roof would do eight years later, Adkisson refused an insanity defense, fearing that it would diminish the legitimacy of his racist and homophobic ideological positions. Instead, he pleaded guilty to murder and was sent to prison for life. His sentencing judge asked the killer if he had anything to say to his victims, but again like Roof he got lockjaw when presented with the opportunity to apologize. "No, ma'am," Adkisson sneered. "I have nothing to say." He did, however, manage to send a message to the tearful UU congregants seated behind him in the courtroom, when he conspicuously used an extended middle finger to scratch the back of his head.

The Southern Poverty Law Center, the civil rights organization based in Montgomery, Alabama, said the Adkisson case "marked yet another deadly incident in a nationwide flurry of right-wing extremist violence and plots in the months leading up to and following the election of the nation's first non-white president."

Roof's Racist Journal

Dylann Roof can be properly regarded as an offshoot of the Adkisson family tree of criminals motivated by racial hatred. He was just 14 years old when Adkisson committed his crimes, but the South Carolinian's own 2,500-word journal betrays several similarities to that of the Tennessean, including subheads that categorize sections based upon a particular brand of bigotry. For Roof, these included "Blacks," "Jews," and "Hispanics." Roof's thoughts were published on his website, "The Last Rhodesian." (The name refers to a lost-cause niche of white-power racists. Roof posted selfies in which he wore jacket patches supporting a return of colonialist white rule to the African country known as Zimbabwe since 1980. Fewer than one percent of the nation's citizens are white.)

Many of the concepts—and even the specific language—of his document were lifted from white supremacist websites. Here are some excerpts. Some typos and punctuations have been fixed to enhance readability, but Roof's own capitalization rules are maintained: White is always uppercase; black, Jew, and Hispanic are relegated to lowercase in the body of his text:

BLACKS

I think it is fitting to start off with the group I have the most real-life experience with, and the group that is the biggest problem for Americans. Niggers are stupid and violent. At the same time, they have the capacity to be very slick. Black people view everything through a racial lens ... They are always thinking about the fact that they are black . . . but White people on average don't think about race in their daily lives. And this is our problem. We need to and have to . . .

I wish with a passion that niggers were treated terribly throughout history by Whites, that every White person had an ancestor who owned slaves, that segregation was an evil and oppressive institution, and so on. Because if it was all true, it would make it so much easier for me to accept our current situation. But it isn't true. None of it is . . .

Segregation was not a bad thing. It was a defensive measure. Segregation did not exist to hold back negroes. It existed to protect us from them . . . Not only did it protect us from having to interact with them, and from being physically harmed by them, but it protected us from being brought down to their level. Integration has done nothing but bring Whites down to the level of brute animals. The best example of this is obviously our school system . . .

Anyone who thinks that White and black people look as different as we do on the outside, but are somehow magically the same on the inside, is delusional. How could our faces, skin, hair, and body structure all be different, but our brains be exactly the same? . . . There are personality traits within human families, and within different breeds of cats or dogs, so why not within the races? . . . Just because we can breed with the other races doesn't make us the same . . .

JEWS

Unlike many White nationalists, I am of the opinion that the majority of American and European jews are White. In my opinion the issue with jews is not their blood, but their identity. I think that if we could somehow destroy the jewish identity, then they wouldn't cause much of a problem. The problem is that jews look White, and in many cases are White, yet they see themselves as minorities. Just like niggers, most jews are always thinking about the fact that they are jewish. The other issue is that they network. If we could somehow turn every jew blue for 24 hours, I think there would be a mass awakening, because people would be able to see plainly what is going on. I don't pretend to understand why jews do what they do. They are enigma.

HISPANICS

Hispanics are obviously a huge problem for Americans. But there are good hispanics and bad hispanics. I remember while watching hispanic television stations, the shows and even the commercials were more White than our own. They have respect for White beauty, and a good portion of hispanics are White. It is a well-known fact that White hispanics make up the elite of most hispanics countries. There is good White blood worth saving in Uruguay, Argentina, Chile and even Brazil. But they are still our enemies . . .

PATRIOTISM

I hate the sight of the American flag. Modern American patriotism is an absolute joke. People pretending like they have something to be proud of while White people are being murdered daily in the streets. Many veterans believe we owe them something for "protecting our way of life" or "protecting our freedom." But I'm not sure what way of life they are talking about. How about we protect the White race and stop fighting for the jews. I will say this though, I myself would have rather lived in 1940s America than Nazi Germany . . . So I don't blame the veterans of any wars up until after Vietnam, because at least they had an America to be proud of and fight for.

AN EXPLANATION

To take a saying from a film [American History X, about a white supremacist], *"I see all this stuff going on, and I don't see anyone doing anything about it. And it pisses me off." To take a saying from my favorite film* [Himizu, a Japanese film centered on two despairing teenagers], *"Even if my life is worth less than a speck of dirt, I want to use it for the good of society." I have no choice. I am not in the position to, alone, go into the ghetto and fight. I chose Charleston because it is the most historic city in my state, and at one time had the highest ratio of blacks to Whites in the country. We have no skinheads, no real*

KKK, no one doing anything but talking on the Internet. Well someone has to have the bravery to take it to the real world, and I guess that has to be me . . .

Racial Radicalization

Roof offered his own account of his racial radicalization. "The event that truly awakened me was the Trayvon Martin case," he wrote. Martin, 17, was the unarmed black youth shot and killed in 2012 in Miami Gardens, Florida, by a neighborhood watch volunteer, George Zimmerman. The shooting and the failure of a jury to hold Zimmerman criminally responsible induced a race-infused furor in the U.S. that persists. Roof, just ten months older than Martin at the time of the shooting, was prompted to "look him up." He explained what happened next:

> *I read the Wikipedia article and right away I was unable to understand what the big deal was. It was obvious that Zimmerman was in the right. But more importantly this prompted me to type in the words "black on White crime" into Google, and I have never been the same since that day. The first website I came to was the Council of Conservative Citizens. There were pages upon pages of these brutal black-on-White murders. I was in disbelief. At this moment I realized that something was very wrong. How could the news be blowing up the Trayvon Martin case while hundreds of these black-on-White murders got ignored?*

From this point I researched deeper and found out what was happening in Europe. I saw that the same things were happening in England and France, and in all the other Western European countries. Again I found myself in disbelief. As an American we are taught to accept living in the melting pot, and black and other minorities have just as much right to be here as we do, since we are all immigrants. But Europe is the homeland of White people, and in many ways the situation is even worse there. From here I found out about the Jewish problem and other issues facing our race, and I can say today that I am completely racially aware.

Roof's introductory source, the Council of Conservative Citizens, is described by the Southern Poverty Law Center as "a crudely racist group that once called black people a 'retrograde species of humanity.'" Among the group's "principles," according to its website:

We believe the United States is a European country and that Americans are part of the European people . . . We also oppose all efforts to mix the races of mankind, to promote non-white races over the European-American people through so-called "affirmative action" and similar measures, to destroy or denigrate the European-American heritage, including the heritage of the Southern people, and to force the integration of the races.

The Anti-Defamation League, a Jewish advocacy group based in New York, reports that the council is prominent among hate groups that post blatantly concocted false reports of black-on-white crime as a propaganda tool to lure in prospective white supremacists. It worked perfectly well with Dylann Roof. Google has changed its algorithms to lower the search profile of such groups, but many still can be found.

At Roof's murder trial, defense attorney David Bruck acknowledged his client's deep bigotry. But he added:

> *Every bit of motivation came from things he saw on the Internet . . . He is simply regurgitating, in whole paragraphs, slogans and facts—bits and pieces of facts that he downloaded from the Internet directly into his brain.*

Refusal to Apologize

That might have drawn sympathy if only Roof—now presumably more informed—had even once apologized. He has not—and pointedly so. He went so far as to draw a white supremacist version of a Celtic Cross—used by neo-Nazis, the KKK, and other racists—on the canvas sneakers he wore to court. Six weeks after the murders, he wrote in a jailhouse journal that his loss of freedom was "worth it."

"I would like to make it crystal clear, I do not regret what I did," Roof wrote. "I am not sorry. I have not shed a tear for the innocent people I killed."

A hometown clergyman who visited Roof frequently behind bars says he remains defiantly racist, and a psychiatrist has diagnosed him with a long list of problems. These include social anxiety disorder, schizoid personality disorder, depression, and possibly some form of autism—which in combination leave him "emotionally flat," according to the expert. But like many criminals, Roof feels he knows better. "There's nothing wrong with me," he told jurors at his trial, against all evidence to the contrary, including the nine corpses.

Dylann Storm Roof, inmate number 28509-171, resides at a stout federal prison a mile from the Wabash River south of Terre Haute, Indiana. He lives on death row there with about 60 other men. Typically, condemned American killers like Roof can expect to live at least ten years while awaiting execution, and many survive for 20 years or more. In one of his musings from behind bars, Roof has suggested that perhaps one day his life will be saved with a pardon by a sympathetic president. That idea would have seemed like a demented fantasy just a few years ago, but amid the political earthquake that has tugged America's currently dominant political party ever closer to the alt-right, who knows what a president might do if he believes it would play well with his loyal base?

Rachel Kaadzi Ghansah, who won the Pulitzer Prize for her 2017 *GQ* magazine profile of Roof's life and crimes, worries that the troubled southern man could be more trend leader than lone wolf in these times.

The rise of groups like Trump's Republican Party, with its overtures to the alt-right, has emboldened men like

Dylann Roof to come out of their slumber and loudly, violently out themselves. But in South Carolina, those men never disappeared, were there always, waiting. It is possible that Dylann Roof is not an outlier at all, then, but rather emblematic of an approaching storm.

Chapter 8.
When Slaughter
Became Ordinary

On an oppressive Miami morning in August 1982, a man named Carl Brown, who had lost his teaching job after going off the rails, asked his adolescent son to join him on an outing. "I'm going to kill a lot of people," he told the boy. The ten-year-old wisely declined to tag along, so Brown set out alone on his bicycle, with an Ithaca 12-gauge shotgun slung across his back and the bike's cargo basket sagging with ammunition. He was bound for a Hialeah, Florida, machine shop, where he had a beef over a $20 lawnmower repair. After settling a score there, he planned to move on to Hialeah Junior High School, where he had been suspended from his longtime teaching position.

The school's principal, Octavio Visiedo, had described Brown as "incoherent" and his classroom as "total and complete chaos." Brown would waste entire class periods babbling an often-bigoted diatribe about whatever came to his troubled mind—

God, sex, black people. He baffled students with blustering tales about how he was God's man-on-earth as the embodiment of Logos, the ancient Grecian philosophical concept of cosmic order, and he interrupted his monologues with crazed chants of: "United States! United States! United States!"

"I also fear for the safety of the students," Visiedo wrote in an evaluation of Brown. "I continue to be alarmed about the potential for disaster in that class."

One of his students later told the press: "He was off his rocker."

Born in Chicago, Brown, 51, moved south after a stint in the Navy. He then earned a teaching degree and went to work in 1962 at Hialeah Junior High, where he was known in his early years as a competent social studies teacher who maintained military-style discipline in class. But year by year and step by step, Brown descended into an abyss of psychosis and grew haggard and gaunt, slumping prematurely into dotage. Students began to rebel against his unhinged soliloquies.

"We come to school to learn, not to hear his problems," one girl complained to school officials in 1977. "How can we learn anything with teachers like that?"

Brown pushed back with batty letters (for "the enlightenment" of school officials) about nonexistent "infancy laws" that he believed sanctioned his supreme classroom authority. School administrators kicked the can down the road by transferring Brown to another school in 1981, but his mental illness only deepened, and he was finally suspended in March 1982, his 20th year of teaching. Dr. Robert Wainger, the psychiatrist he was assigned to see, diagnosed grandiosity, paranoia, and a "sexual fixation." However, two days before Brown's armed bike ride, Wainger judged Brown unfit to return to teaching but concluded he was not dangerous. His patient would prove him dead wrong.

Mower Repair Was a Tipping Point

In the midst of his occupational crisis, Brown's second marriage was disintegrating because he ignored his wife's insistence that he get help. The picayune conflict with Bob Moore's Welding Shop was a tipping point. Brown was unhappy with a minor mower repair and was angered that the shop had refused to accept a traveler's check as payment. After bickering with employees there on August 18 he then stalked out, muttering threats. He returned on August 20 aboard his bike and stormed inside. Brandishing the shotgun he bought the day before, Brown blazed his way through the office area and onto the repair floor, pumping two point-blank shots at anyone he encountered, then reloading.

A local cop said: "He came in and just went nuts."

By the time he was finished, Brown had killed eight and wounded three in the shop. With 20 shells remaining in his arsenal, he pointed his bicycle toward his old school, but two Good Samaritans interceded. Mike Kram and Ernest Hammett, who worked near Moore's shop, chased him down with a car. Kram shot Brown in the back with a pistol, then used his auto to propel him into a concrete stanchion, killing him.

Most Americans will not recall Carl Brown's eight-fatality assault, but in 1982 he was major national news. His crime had the highest body count of any shooting in Florida history, although it has been outdone several times in more recent years. The shooting was a shock to South Florida, and it led to a rare political initiative. Five weeks after the murders, the Hialeah City Council voted 6–1 to enact a meager, three-day waiting period to buy rifles and shotguns. But three weeks later, the same council rescinded the ordinance after local gun dealers complained that the law was killing their business. The short-lived regulation was a herald of the political quagmire that encompassed any attempt to enact a firearms regulation, however modest, in the U.S.

Many gun violence archives use the Brown case as the starting point for their tallies of contemporary American mass killings. Brown was a trend-setter in several regards. Investigators found a leading-edge example of a mad murderer's manifesto on a cassette tape at his home.

"This is Logos speaking," Brown intoned. "God through me is responsible for the good and bad sounds in your head . . . I am indestructible on Earth."

Cases That Reset Our Sensibilities

The machine shop slaughter was the first of eight U.S. murder cases in the 1980s with at least six killed, and the American mass murder graph has pointed upward ever since. Precise enumeration is challenging because federal law enforcement agencies—kept on a short leash by politicians who quake before the gun lobby—have until recently made no real attempt to keep an official record of mass shootings. As a result, non-official counts vary widely. But the trend that began in the 1980s clearly continued

And then it got worse . . . A spontaneous outpouring of grief outside Pulse nightclub, Orlando, where Omar Mateen had just killed 49 people, topping the number of casualties at Virginia Tech.

in the 1990s, when 11 shootings that claimed six or more lives were recorded, including the stunning carnage at Colorado's Columbine High School. From 2000 to 2010, the U.S. witnessed 15 shootings with at least six fatalities, notably including a record 32 killed at Virginia Tech in 2007.

And then it got worse. The next decade in the sequence brought one numbing case after another as killers treated casualty counts like points on a scoreboard. The Virginia Tech record was topped twice in just 16 months—49 killed at an Orlando, Florida, nightclub in June 2016, then 58 in Las Vegas on October 1, 2017. Three of the five most deadly mass shootings occurred in an 18-month stretch, including those two cases and the 26 killed ten weeks after Las Vegas at a Texas church. Mass murder in America now seems to be an inevitability, not an anomaly. And it should shock no one when someone comes along to dethrone the king of the hill, Stephen Paddock, the enigmatic Las Vegas shooter.

I believe that a cluster of three cases in 2011 and 2012— shocking, large-scale murders perpetrated by Jared Loughner, James Holmes, and Adam Lanza—reset our sensibilities about the ineluctability of mass carnage. Decades ago, blue-ribbon government committees examined these sorts of cases and published vast, guileless reports that concluded with earnest recommendations about how to prevent such atrocities from happening again. Often those recommendations focused on access to guns, a subject that has been politically verboten for more than 20 years now. Since 2011, I have watched this sensibility shift. We now seem to regard mass shootings as a Leviathan that no one—not citizens, not law enforcers, and certainly not politicians—can stop. We hunker down and wait for the next one—and hope it happens in some other place, far from our loved ones.

The attacks by Loughner, Holmes, and Lanza were public mass shootings at the sort of places that most of us visit regularly—a grocery store, a movie theater, a school. Nearly all of the victims were random targets with no relationship to the shooters. They were in the wrong place at the wrong time, as the bromide goes. That is the twin terror of these three shootings: ordinary places, ordinary people. Some experts, notably Northeastern University's James Alan Fox, argue that mass killings are rare events undeserving of what they see as overblown "moral panic." That may be a scientifically accurate position, but it's also a tough sell in a country that has witnessed the escalating death tolls of spree killers. Whether warranted or not, terror-inducing killers like Loughner, Holmes, and Lanza have left many Americans looking over their shoulders, fearing it could happen to any of them in a luckless moment.

Jared Loughner

Jared Loughner looks like a proud young man in the mugshot taken by Pima County, Arizona, sheriff's personnel a short time after he joined the club of American mass killers. He wears a smile—or perhaps a smirk—with his left jaw crinkled with grin lines. His deep-set brown eyes seem to glow. On January 8, 2011, Loughner showed up at a Saturday morning meet-and-greet outside a Safeway grocery story in Tucson, Arizona, for Gabby Giffords, a Democratic member of Congress who represented that city in Washington, D.C. At 10:10 a.m., as Loughner stood fewer than 10 ft (3 m) from the politician, he drew a 9mm Glock pistol and shot her in the head. He then fired random shots at the 30 people assembled around her. Loughner was tackled to the ground when he paused to install a fresh 33-round magazine.

How did Loughner manage to get hold of a gun legally with his record of drug and alcohol abuse, depression, and bizarre behavior?

His bullets had found the flesh of 21 victims. Six were killed, including a federal judge, a young Giffords aide, and a nine-year-old girl who had gone to the event with a friend to meet the congresswoman. Giffords herself was critically injured but survived. (She has become one of the country's most fierce and credible gun control advocates.) As Loughner was led away by police, he seemed to imagine himself playing a role— Jimmy Cagney in a Warner Bros. shoot-'em-up.

"I plead the Fifth," he declared.

In short order by U.S. justice standards, Loughner also pleaded guilty, which likely allowed him to cheat the proverbial hangman. He was sent to prison and is unlikely to ever live free again.

The key backstory to this case, as with so many, is the question of how in the world this man managed to legally own a gun. Loughner was a mess. He abused alcohol and drugs, had been rejected as an enlistee for military service, and had been tossed from college due to bizarre behavior. A psychologist testified that Loughner was a schizophrenic who had been depressed since his mid-teens. Yet six weeks before the shooting, on November 30, 2010, he was able to walk into a Tucson franchise of Sportsman's Warehouse, a national sporting goods chain, and walk out carrying a deadly weapon under highly permissive Arizona gun laws. He bought his ammunition at Walmart a few hours before the shooting.

Three days after the murders, Loughner's parents released a statement in which they said: "We don't understand why this happened." Perhaps they were unfamiliar with their son, because he left a clear record online of maniacal paranoia and delusion. His writings are spiced with bizarre observations about talking birds and the political importance of grammar, and he often expressed his beliefs with nonsensical if/then statements—if this, then that—familiar to college students from introductory classes in logic. Here are examples from one post:

> *If there's no flag in the constitution then the flag in the*
> *film is unknown.*
> *There's no flag in the constitution.*
> *Therefore, the flag in the film is unknown . . .*

> *If you protest the government then there's a new*
> *government from protesting.*
> *There's not a new government from protesting.*
> *Thus, you aren't protesting the government.*

Obsessed by the Illegitimacy of Government

He was obsessed with what he saw as the illegitimacy of government and its currency. Here is a transcript of one of his YouTube videos:

> *Hello, my name is Jared Lee Loughner.*
> *This video is my introduction to you! My favorite*
> *activity is conscience dreaming; the greatest inspiration*
> *for my political business information. Some of you don't*
> *dream—sadly.*
> *Firstly, the current government officials are in*
> *power for their currency, but I'm informing you for*

your new currency! If you're treasurer of a new money system, then you're responsible for the distributing of a new currency . . . As a result, the people approve a new money system which is promising new information that's accurate, and we truly believe in a new currency. Above all, you have your new currency, listener?

Secondly, my hope is for you to be literate! . . . The majority of people who reside in District 8 [Tucson's congressional district] are illiterate—hilarious. I don't control your English grammar structure, but you control your English grammar structure.

Thirdly, I know who's listening: government officials and the people. Nearly all the people, who don't know this accurate information of a new currency, aren't aware of mind control and brainwash methods . . .

In conclusion, my ambition is for informing literate dreamers about a new currency; in a few days, you know I'm conscience dreaming! Thank you!

In another video, "My Final Thoughts," Loughner applied his if/then conditional statements to a series of issues, from calendar calculations to terrorism to grammar. A sample:

If 987,123,478,961,876,341,234,098,601,978,618 is the year in B.C.E. then the previous year is 987,123,478,961, 876,341,234,098,601,978,619 B.C.E.

987,123,478,961,876,341,234,098,601,978,618 is the year in B.C.E.

Therefore, the previous year of 987,123,478,961,87 6,341,234,098,601,978,619 B.C.E ...

If you call me a terrorist, then the argument to call me a terrorist is Ad hominem.

You call me a terrorist.

Thus, the argument to call me a terrorist is Ad hominem ...

In conclusion, reading the second United States Constitution, I can't trust the current government because of the ratifications: The government is implying mind control and brainwash on the people by controlling grammar.

No! I won't pay debt with a currency that's not backed by gold and silver!

No! I won't trust in God! What's government if words don't have meaning?

Strange as it might have been, that last question is pertinent to Loughner's murders. After the Tucson shooting, a friend of Loughner told Nick Baumann of *Mother Jones* that the killer had harbored a long grudge against Giffords because she had inadequately answered that precise query during a meeting in 2007. The friend, Bryce Tierney, said of Loughner: "He told me that she opened up the floor for questions and he asked a question. The question was: 'What is government if words have no meaning?'"

He was angry at Giffords' reply.

"He said, 'Can you believe it, they wouldn't answer my question,' and I told him, 'Dude, no one's going to answer that.' Ever since that, he thought she was fake. He had something against her."

Classmate Saw Loughner as a Threat

Loughner compiled a list of his favorite books on his YouTube profile—*Animal Farm, Brave New World, The Wizard of Oz, One Flew Over the Cuckoo's Nest*, and others. We parse these "favorites" lists, which have become common from mass killers, for insight, but the primary takeaway is just how deeply troubled Jared Loughner was. His community college classmates recognized it from day one. In a note she made following her first math class with Loughner in 2010, one student wrote:

> We do have one student in the class who was disruptive today. I'm not certain yet if he was on drugs (as one person surmised) or disturbed. He scares me a bit. The teacher tried to throw him out and he refused to go, so I talked to the teacher afterward. Hopefully he will be out of class very soon, and not come back with an automatic weapon.

The same student added two weeks later:

> He is one of those whose picture you see on the news, after he has come into class with an automatic weapon.

Politician Gabby Giffords was shot in the head at close range with a Glock pistol by Jared Loughner.

> *Everyone interviewed would say, "Yeah, he was in my math class and he was really weird." I sit by the door with my purse handy. If you see it on the news one night, know that I got out fast . . .*

The only thing she got wrong was the venue.

Several other examples of mass violence happened in 2011 and 2012, including deadly rampages with five to eight victims each in a Minneapolis workplace shooting; two cases related to domestic discord at a spa in Georgia and a hair salon in California; restaurant shootings in Seattle, Washington, and Carson City, Nevada; a shooting by a disgruntled former student at an Oakland, California, college; and a racist attack on a Sikh temple near Milwaukee, Wisconsin. Beyond the locales where they took place, most of these barely raised a blip on the national crime consciousness scale—a sign of mass murder ho-hum. But the Colorado theater shooting by James Holmes, examined in the previous chapter, certainly attracted attention, both at home and abroad. The venue and the randomness were mortifying: Who hasn't visited the same sort of multiplex?

Adam Lanza

And then came Adam Lanza's assault on Connecticut first-graders, five months after the movie massacre, on December 14, 2012. I was visiting a prison in New York's Catskill Mountains that day, speaking to a class of inmates, all aspiring writers, who were being taught by my friend Bruce Porter, a fellow word-hurler whose work also focuses on con men and crime. After exiting the prison, Bruce and I stopped for a beer and watched CNN's coverage of the Sandy Hook School slaughter on a TV mounted behind the bar. We were mostly speechless, but Bruce managed this insight: "We've reached the point of no return, haven't we?" It seemed at that moment as though the Rubicon was in our rear-view mirror and that the American disease of mass murder had yoked us all. As Lanza's father, Peter, would later say: "I want people to be afraid of the fact that this could happen to them."

Adam Lanza, born in 1992, was the second son of Peter, an accounting executive, and his spouse, Nancy, a stockbroker who gave up her career to raise their child. He was an unusual kid—mute until age three and emotionally repressed as he grew up. Speaking to *The New Yorker* in 2014, Peter Lanza described his son as "always thinking differently. Just a normal little weird kid." Adam was diagnosed with Asperger's syndrome as an

Many thought Adam Lanza harmless, but his obsession with school shootings was getting worse and worse.

adolescent, although the boy rejected that medical judgment. A middle school teacher called young Lanza "intelligent but not normal, with anti-social issues."

He became increasingly hypersensitive to noises, colors, light, human touch, germs, even certain fabrics, refused to wear clothing that had tags of any kind, and complained of odors that no one else could discern. Sensory overload manifested itself in other strange ways: Vivid color graphics in textbooks overwhelmed him, for example; his mother copied the pages in black and white. He was diagnosed with sensory integration disorder, a condition sometimes associated with autism.

These various obstacles to learning led Nancy Lanza to enroll her son in a series of schools, trying to find one that suited his special needs. (Lanza had attended the Sandy Hook School until sixth grade.) Ultimately, he withdrew in tenth grade, at about the time his parents' marriage ended, and was homeschooled by his mother. By then he had developed panic attacks, crying jags, a bug-eyed stare, a stiff-legged gait, and a tendency to stay locked up in his room. His mother arranged psychiatric counseling, but his impassivity was a roadblock. He tried the anti-depressant Lexapro, but his mother wrote that the drug left him "practically vegetative . . . He did nothing but sit in his dark room staring at nothing."

Cruel though it may seem, some have criticized Nancy Lanza—Adam's first murder victim on the day of his spree—for enabling her son's dysfunction by trying to cocoon him from irritations. She also made the puzzling decision to transfer to Adam her own enthusiasm for firearms. He accompanied her on regular visits to a gun club—no doubt because it was one way to get him out of his bedroom, where he kept the curtains drawn and the lights out. Like many pseudocommando mass shooters, Lanza grew fascinated with guns and military history. He dreamed of joining the elite Army Rangers, although he hadn't a prayer of achieving the physical demands required.

Online Forum Posts

A few days after Christmas 2009, the 17-year-old Lanza used the screen name "Smiggles" to join an online forum focused on a controversial role-playing game, "Super Columbine Massacre RPG," in which players assume the identities of the Columbine killers. The name of the forum was later changed to "Shocked Beyond Belief"—derived from a comment Eric Harris made on video just before he attacked his high school—and the subject broadened to spree killings in general. In 296 posts over the ensuing 22 months, Lanza revealed himself to be a scholar of mass killings—his initial posts showed off a deep knowledge of films about spree murders, both documentary and fiction. Later, he shared with forum-mates a massive spreadsheet he had compiled—a "comprehensive list of mass murderers and their attributes"—which police would later find in his home. It included some 500 cases. Psychologists have suggested that Lanza used this research to rationalize—or even normalize—his fixation on mass murder.

His forum posts show Lanza to have been clever, intelligent, and cordially combative. He also displayed a bit of whimsy. On April 20, 2010—coincidentally, the 11th anniversary of Columbine—Lanza posted a comment on a thread entitled "What is fun?" "Hamsters," Lanza wrote. "Everything about them is amazing." In another post, he wrote that he had dreamed about Columbine, recounting a surreal nightmare in which he was confronted by "a huge purple monster with long arms." He was sufficiently self-aware to recognize his own pendulum-like mood swings and psychotic episodes, including occasional hallucinations of "distorted faces flashing through my mind." On Christmas Day 2011 he wrote:

> *I was as depressed as I get during my last post, and I'm fine with the interminable depression that I normally have, but now I'm incoherently giddy with glee. Well, relative to my baseline . . . Except now that I'm giddy, I can't really say that I hate it because I think everything is delightful. If depressives cut themselves to feel better, I*

wonder what cutting a happy-go-lucker would do. Santa's supposed to be jolly. I hope he visits me tonight so I can find out.

Two days later, his yoyo mood was back down. Commenting on a thread about New Year's resolutions, he wrote: "Pfft, goals are artificial impositions of deprivation. I'm content to mope on the floor 24/7."

Lanza had a number of peculiar fixations, including Travis, an aging former show business chimpanzee who was shot dead by police in Connecticut in February 2009 after he mauled a woman. Lanza felt deep sympathy for the animal and seemed to identify with him, to the extent that the chimp's death led to one of the most evocative records of Lanza's mindset. The teenager was a regular listener (via online streaming) of *Anarchy Radio*, a University of Oregon show hosted by John Zerzan, an anarchist and primitivist philosopher. Zerzan professes that the alienation of modern life has had a calamitous psychological effect on humans, and he used his radio show to highlight cases of extreme violence to support that supposition. He explained the concept in his book *Future Primitive Revisited*:

> *There are more and more "narcissistically troubled" people, products of the lovelessness and extreme alienation of modern divided society, and its cultural and spiritual impoverishment. Deep feelings of emptiness characterize the narcissist, coupled with a boundless rage, often just under the surface, at the sense*

of dependency felt because of dominated life, and the hollowness of one starved by a deficient reality.

In December 2011, Lanza phoned Zerzan's show to suggest that the chimp was a non-human embodiment of the same violence-inducing alienation. Speaking in a flat drone, Lanza gave Zerzan the essential background details of the chimp's attack, then went on virtually uninterrupted for seven minutes. Here are excerpts:

> *And this might not seem very relevant, but I'm bringing it up because afterward, everyone was condemning his owner for saying how irresponsible she was for raising a chimp like it was a child. And that she should have known something like this would happen, because chimps aren't supposed to be living in civilization, they're supposed to be living in the wild, among each other . . . And it's easy to say there's something wrong with it simply because it's a chimp, but what's the real difference between us and our closest relatives? Travis wasn't an untamed monster at all. He wasn't just feigning domestication, he was civilized. . . .*
>
> *But anyway, look what civilization did to him: it had the same exact effect on him as it has on humans. He was profoundly sick, in every sense of the term, and he had to resort to these surrogate activities like watching baseball, and looking at pictures on a computer screen, and taking Xanax. He was a complete mess. And his*

attack wasn't simply because he was a senselessly
violent, impulsive chimp, which was how his behavior
was universally portrayed . . . Some little thing he
experienced was the last straw, and he was overwhelmed
by the life that he had, and he wanted to get out of it by
changing his environment . . .

His attack can be seen entirely parallel to the
attacks and random acts of violence that you bring
up on your show every week—committed by humans,
which the mainstream also has no explanation for . . .
I just don't think it would be such a stretch to say that
he very well could have been a teenage mall shooter or
something like that.

As Lanza finished, Zernan said: "Wow. Very well articulated."

Posting as Smiggles online, Lanza suggested a kinship with poor Travis, writing: "My wet dream is living in the wild with apes." Instead, he lived in utter solitude in a cave-like bedroom. In the final year of his life, he ventured outside so infrequently that his car battery died after sitting idle for months. His posts suggest deep despair. As he wrote late one night: "I spent all day ruminating over how much I hate culture. Now I've calmed down and am left lying on the floor, numbly perplexed over the foreign concept of loving life." Here is a post from October 2010:

On another tangent, what do you think about sunlight?
Those drapes haven't been opened in the last five years,
and the drapes in the room I'm in right now have actually

been taped shut (to block the gaps from allowing sunlight through) for the same amount of time. I absolutely hate sunlight, along with any artificial light which resembles it. The few times I see an extremely bleak, dark, and dreary day outside during the morning or afternoon with thick gray clouds covering the entire sky, I get into a good mood and think about how wonderfully beautiful it is outside. Bright, sunny, "cheerful" days are depressing. Nearly every afternoon is miserable for me. Beyond just the normal animosity I have for sunlight, I get exhausted between noon and sunset when I'm in a room which allows the slightest amount of afternoon light in. I hate having my skin exposed to sunlight, so I always wear a hooded sweatshirt and full-length pants, even in the hottest weather . . . I would also wear a full balaclava if it wouldn't get me profiled as a criminal. They need to make a fashion come-back.

On January 11, 2011, three days after Jared Loughner's attack in Arizona, Lanza posted an analysis in the forum, saying that Loughner:

apparently is one of the very few mass murderers who is legitimately delusional (although I haven't completely determined that yet; crimes which receive a lot of media attention sort of irritate me and I usually defer reading about them for a while).

He continued:

> *The way which this particular incident is being treated is frustrating to me. Jiverly Voong* [better known as Wong, a mass shooter in Binghamton, New York] *inflicted a similar number of casualties with more than double the deaths not too long ago, and he was virtually ignored compared to this. I hate how the lives of state-sanctioned thugs* [a reference to Rep. Giffords] *are treated as if they're more valuable than that of anyone else.*

Lanza had strident opinions about which killers deserved attention, and he frequently edited Wikipedia entries about them. He seemed to believe that insanity disqualified Loughner from serious media attention, and he flashed his scholar's chops by comparing Loughner to Wong. He had a point.

A delusional naturalized American citizen from Vietnam, Wong, 41, believed that police had been spying on him for years and were transmitting messages into his brain. He killed 13 people at a Binghamton immigration center in 2009 before committing suicide. With a body count of victims equal to Columbine, Wong's massacre was a one-day story for the national media.

In another post, Lanza noted: "Dead people in general receive more respect and blind compassion than they ever would have while alive. I don't understand it." He also opined that mass shooters whose motives are a "mystery" tend to get more attention. No doubt it was not a coincidence that he destroyed his computer before launching his attack, forcing investigators and journalists to sweep up clues of his motivations from footprints left online. Stephen Paddock, the Las Vegas killer, used the same strategy, scrubbing his identity both online and off.

With his encyclopedic knowledge of the subject, Lanza could be an astute critic of media portrayals of mass murder. In October 2011, he commented online about the arrest of an 11-year-old girl who briefly made the national news after threatening her school. Lanza thought it was frivolous for the media to report an unconvincing threat by an adolescent. "She's obviously an Andrew Golden copykitten," he wrote. "These incidents would stop happening if it weren't for overzealous reporters publicizing them." (Golden, also 11, and his pal Mitchell Johnson, 13, had killed five people and wounded ten in an Arkansas school shooting more than 25 years earlier.) Lanza also mocked a school-shooter episode of the American TV drama *Homicide: Life on the Street*, for its ham-handed plot driven by predictable dialogue. He sarcastically summarized: "This tragedy could have been prevented. Steve showed all of the warning signs."

He shared a list of creepy movies—his favorite death scenes and a compilation of mass murder documentaries or feature films adapted from true crime cases—and he often added informed but quirky commentary. This was his mini-review of an old film about a serial killer who targeted young brunettes. Some plot points reminded Lanza of Charles Whitman, the 1996 Texas Tower killer, and he used that connection to goose the media's theories about the effects of violent entertainment on murder-minded men:

Today I saw The Sniper *(1952), which was released when Charles Whitman was still a wee Boy Scout, but the main character was more of a serial killer. Despite that disappointment, it was still excellent and presciently anticipated future psychological horrors. Now that I think of it, I'm sure that Charles Whitman must have snuck into a showing of* The Sniper *and eventually ended up imitating what he saw. After all, the sniper in the movie used a variant of an M1 carbine, which was one of the rifles that was brought up the Austin tower. What has the media done to our children?*

In February 2012, Lanza displayed his granular knowledge in a 650-word essay that was his final post on the forum. He was prompted when another member wrote:

Fact is: school shootings are not common occasions and have steadily decreased from their peak. It is incredibly debatable whether or not societal factors had an effect or in some way influenced Columbine, and to be honest I think it wouldn't have made any difference if the high school was a utopia. I see it as two teenagers who were not well in any sense of the word acting for little to no reason whatsoever.

Lanza fired back:

Columbine wasn't an isolated incident: it was the apex of a string of school shootings which began increasing . . . in the early 1990s. Despite American students committing fewer school shootings in 2000-2009 than they did in 1990-1999, the rate of attempts actually increased beyond their pre-Columbine level. Columbine caused Americans to begin taking the potential for school shootings seriously, and thus many attempts which were expected to have been carried out have instead been prevented. And since 1999, there has been an increase in foreign school massacres . . .

He went on to add global scope, like a good scholar:

. . . It's myopic to telescope on school shootings when they've comprised a small percentage of the larger trend of mass murders, which are carried out in all sorts of contexts; but they always occur in contexts which involve some permutation of alienation, which has been part and parcel with societal "progress." This relationship can be seen with the Chinese mass stabbings. There were some sparse incidents throughout the 20th century, but the rate began to rise in the 1990s and erupted in the early 2000s, corresponding to China's rapid "economic development," culminating in the infamous spate of elementary school stabbings of 2010.

American mass murders were less prevalent before Richard Speck [the Chicago nurse killer] precipitated their rise in 1966 . . . Mass murdering is so ridiculously over-the-top . . . that very few people are prone to do it under any circumstances. But just look at how many fans you can find for all different types of mass murderers— not just the Reb & VoDKa Bunch [Columbine's Harris and Klebold] . . .

Thinking of this society as the default state of existence is the reason why you think that humans would be "not well" for "no reason whatsoever." . . . When civilization exists in a form where all forms of alienation (among many other things) are rampant, as can be seen in the most recent incarnation within the last fifty years . . . , new children will end up "not well" in all sorts of ways.

Sandy Hook Killings

Ten months later, at age 20, Adam Lanza joined the tribe of the mass killers he had studied. His pipedreams of joining the Army Rangers or attending prestigious Cornell University had evaporated, and he had failed as a student at two ordinary local colleges. Early in the morning on Friday, December 14, 2012, Lanza left his bedroom cave and ambushed his mother while she was still in bed, killing her with four shots in the head—three of them redundant. (His father, Peter, with whom he had become estranged, would later say that the four shots were symbolic— one each for mom, dad, brother Ryan, and himself.)

He then collected four of his mother's firearms, including two Bushmaster assault rifles and two handguns, and drove five miles (8 km) to Sandy Hook Elementary School. Dressed in black and wearing earplugs and a tactical vest laden with extra magazines, he arrived at 9:35 a.m. and shot his way through a glass panel in the locked front entrance. First, he killed the school's principal and the school psychologist, who had gone to investigate the initial shot, and then he moved to a first-grade classroom, where substitute teacher Lauren Rousseau—alerted by a custodian— was in the midst of herding her 15 pupils into a bathroom for safety. Lanza fired dozens of shots, killing everyone in the room—the kids, Rousseau, and a behavioral therapist. He then proceeded to an adjacent classroom, where he killed teacher Victoria Soto and five more students.

Miraculously, 11 children survived—some by running out of the room, and others protected by Soto and her aide, Anne Marie Murphy, who also was killed. Police officers arrived just four minutes after the carnage began, in time to hear one final shot. Lanza, standing in classroom 10, used a Glock pistol to shoot himself in the head. He had killed six adults at the school, all of them women, as well as 12 girls and eight boys, each of them six or seven years old. He fired as many as 100 shots with the Bushmaster, and all but two of the victims suffered multiple gunshot wounds.

What would possess this fractured young man to attack first-graders? In the media echo chamber, he was said to have taken his motive "to his grave." *The New Yorker*'s Andrew Solomon characterized him as "a terrorist for an unknowable cause." Some have suggested that he acted out a psychotic version of *The Catcher in the Rye* syndrome—that he was saving children from the life of misery that he had led. James Knoll, a forensic psychiatrist in Syracuse, New York, has asserted that Lanza's massacre was an act of emotional transference: "I carry profound hurt. I'll go ballistic and transfer it onto you." And here is the assessment of Pennsylvania psychologist Peter Langman, the school shooting expert:

> *Adam Lanza remains an enigmatic figure, and his motivations for murder are elusive. He might have had paranoid delusions about children, envied them their social ease and perceived happiness, or been sexually attracted to them. He might have blamed his mother for indoctrinating him with culture, resented her behavior in one or more ways, or killed her for a reason that we cannot guess. Because he experienced psychotic symptoms, his motivation could have been based on a delusion or driven by voices commanding him to kill.*

Was Sexuality a Motive?

Lanza was sufficiently self-aware to have recognized his utter failure as he stood on the cusp of adulthood. He was jobless, had no friends, and lived alone in the dark. Langman hinted at sexuality as a motive, and I'm surprised that this hasn't been explored more fully. The best evidence we have of the twists in Lanza's id comes from a long post he shared with a group of online friends. He sent the message on November 1, 2010, at age 18, and it provided the longest look we have inside the child-killer's mind. You might be surprised by what it reveals:

Ever since I was 14, the entire subject of gay rights which is so pervasive in this society has frustrated me. It's not owing to any malice I have toward homosexuals, but instead is caused by the absurdity of the overwhelming fervor against the discrimination of homosexuals while there is another class of people who genuinely suffer from persecution for their lifestyle. While many people celebrate homosexual relationships, sexual relationships between adults and children are universally condemned and vilified. Every adult who is known to have been involved in one is automatically branded for life as a violent and dangerous rapist. . . . If . . . this applied to homosexuals, the public would be appalled, yet no one cares when it applies to pedophiles . . .

Children would not be "scarred" by their voluntary sexual experiences any more than adults in typical sexual relationships would be "scarred" unless their society shamed them into believing that they should feel guilty. . . .

Why is this society so adamantly opposed to pedophilia? Children deserve all of the rights and respects that an adult should receive, yet this is not the case to any extent. . . . The right of children to have sexual relationships is a small step toward liberating them from the oppression of adults which they currently endure . . .

I know that I will be accused of desiring sexual contact with children, and there might possibly be accusations that I have already had it, but neither case is true. I also have not seen any degree of child pornography (nor intentionally seen any adult pornography). . . . I'm pretty confused when it comes to my sexuality, but I'm certain that I'm not a pedophile.

Chapter 9.
The Viking King of Overkill

Anders Breivik, the homicidal, Islamophobic Norwegian, declared himself "Justiciar Knight Commander for Knights Templar Europe." But he earned a more exalted honorific: He was the king of overkill.

Disturbed by what he called "the ongoing Islamic colonization of Europe," he first murdered eight people with a fertilizer van bomb in the government quarter of Oslo, Norway, and then drove 25 miles (40 km) west and north from Oslo to Lake Tyri. There—dressed in a phony police uniform and armed with a Ruger assault rifle and a Glock pistol—he took a short boat ride to bucolic Utøya island, where dozens of teenagers were enjoying summer camp. For nearly two hours Breivik stalked over the wooded, 26-acre grounds, shooting every human being he found.

"Don't be shy!" he taunted them sadistically. "Come out and play with me!"

He had expended his ammunition, executing 69 more innocent souls, by the time the slow-footed authorities arrived. That morning, July 22, 2011, he had emailed electronic copies of a gargantuan manifesto—more overkill—to hundreds of email addresses, many of them fellow Muslim-hating Facebook friends.

Phantom Revolution

As with so many mass killers, Breivik was besotted by the template narcissist's fantasy that he was lighting the fuse on an explosive

On the day of his attacks, Breivik published a crazed "manifesto" attacking Islam and blaming feminism for destroying Europe's culture.

revolution. But there was no movement, no Knights Templar Europe. He was a lone wolf, and he was writing to himself when he offered "execution" tips to his imagined minions:

> *There are situations in which cruelty is necessary, and refusing to apply necessary cruelty is a betrayal of the people whom you wish to protect . . . Once you decide to strike, it is better to kill too many than not enough, or you risk reducing the desired ideological impact of the strike. Explain what you have done (in an announcement distributed prior to operation) and make certain that everyone understands that we, the free peoples of Europe, are going to strike again and again. Do not apologize, make excuses or express regret for you are acting in self-defense or in a preemptive manner . . . Some innocent will die in our operations as they are simply at the wrong place at the wrong time. Get used [to] the idea. The needs of the many will always surpass the needs of the few.*

Breivik's dissertation, "A European Declaration of Independence," is not entirely original. As he admits, about half the content is copied-and-pasted from other sources, mostly racist, right-wing correspondents from Europe and the U.S. Reading the document is a commitment—it runs to nearly a million words—but toss a dart at any of those 1,515 single-spaced pages and it likely will land on a paragraph filled with madness, whose fulcrum point is what he calls "the ongoing genocide of the Nordic tribes."

Scores of pages are dedicated to disquisitions by Breivik and his contributors on the question of whether or not the Islamic faith deserves a place among the world's great faiths (they agree it does not); whether its oracles deserve credit as great leaders and thinkers (ditto); and how Christianity stacks up in comparison.

"A lot of people believe today that Christianity still is and was as evil as Islam?!" Breivik declares. "I can attest to the fact that this is absolutely incorrect." So there you have it.

Parallels in U.S. Racism

Breivik offers a middlebrow version of the trailer park bigotry of Dylann Roof, the white supremacist who killed nine African Americans in 2015 at a South Carolina church. Roof's mission statement was brief by comparison—Breivik's table of contents covers more pages than the South Carolinian's entire monograph—but like Breivik, Roof was preoccupied with white superiority. He oozed old-fashioned southern racism with passages like this: "Niggers are stupid and violent . . . Negroes have lower IQs, lower impulse control, and higher testosterone levels in general."

"Higher testosterone" is emblematic of the white sexual insecurity etched in the lurid American history of Jim Crow laws and the lynching of blacks, both rooted in nativist revulsion over miscegenation, racial "impurity," and what academicians call the "hypermasculinized phallicity" of black men. That racist stink lingers. As Roof wrote: "I have noticed a great disdain for race-mixing White women within the White nationalist community, bordering on insanity. These women are victims, and they can be saved." That disdain has been in plain view in the U.S. for centuries. Mixed-race couples still face scrutinizing stares, the daggers of casual racism. I see it often, and I felt it once while working as a journalist in my hometown of Omaha, Nebraska. While I was walking along a busy corridor in a government building with a source, an assistant court clerk who was a black woman, the heads of rubberneckers whipped around as we passed. It was absurd. "Do you see this happening?" I said to the woman. "All the time," she replied.

Political Support for Racist Behavior

But why wouldn't they stare? Americans have been well-conditioned by their politicians, such as an infamous racist diatribe in 1907 by Ben Tillman, a U.S. senator (and former governor) from Roof's home state. Tillman stood before Congress and argued in favor of lynching, declaring that the sexual threat of demonic black men against white women required the abandonment of constitutional protections:

> *The white women of the South are in a state of siege . . . Some lurking demon who has watched for the opportunity seizes her: she is choked or beaten into insensibility and ravished, her body prostituted, her purity destroyed, her chastity taken from her, and a memory branded on her brain as with a red-hot iron to haunt her night and day as long as she lives . . . Shall men cold-bloodedly stand up and demand for him the right to have a fair trial and be punished in the regular course*

of justice? . . . Civilization peels off us, any and all of us
who are men, and we revert to the original savage type
whose impulses under any and all such circumstances
has always been to kill! kill! kill!

And kill they did. In its heartbreaking investigation of more than 4,000 racial terror lynchings in the South from the Civil War to the 1940s, the Equal Justice Initiative, a civil rights organization based in Montgomery, Alabama, found that many of the murders "resulted from a wildly distorted fear of interracial sex." That paranoia was woven into the American school integration battles of the 1950s and 1960s. Walter Givhan, a prominent white Alabama politician, called school race-mixing a campaign "to open the bedroom doors of our white women to Negro men."

In his diatribe, Tillman described blacks as monkey-like and said the South was being "engulfed, as it were, in a black flood of semi-barbarians." The demonization and animalization of people of color survives today. In June 2018, amid the unceasingly contentious debate about Mexican border security, the president of the United States tweeted: "Big mistake made all over Europe in allowing millions of people in who have so strongly and violently changed their culture!" He added: "We don't want what is happening with immigration in Europe to happen with us!" The next day, he followed by wielding a word usually reserved for vermin: "They [Democrats] don't care about crime and want illegal immigrants, no matter how bad they may be, to pour into and infest our Country . . ."

These might have been career-ending comments for an American politician—Democrat or Republican—just a few years ago. Today, abhorrent racism has become a red alert issue for paleoconservatives: Whiteness is in demographic danger. Patrick Buchanan, the irascible grandfather of that tribe, picked up on Donald Trump's theme in a blog post: "How does the West, America included, stop the flood tide of migrants before it alters forever the political and demographic character of our nations and our civilization?" He expounded further on a conservative radio show:

> *This is the great issue of our time. And the real question is whether Europe has the will and the capacity, and America has the capacity, to halt the invasion of the countries until they change the character—political, social, racial, ethnic—of the country entirely. You cannot stop these sentiments of people who want to live together with their own, and they want their borders protected.*

This anti-brown message has leached into the Republican ideological mainstream. Here's how Trump's acolyte and defender Laura Ingraham, a Fox News host, put it on her TV program in August 2018:

> *It does seem like the America we know and love doesn't exist anymore. Massive demographic changes have been foisted on the American people. And they are changes that none of us ever voted for, and most of us don't like.*

*From Virginia to California, we see stark examples of
how radically, in some ways, the country has changed.
Now much of this is related to both illegal and legal
immigration that, of course, progressives love.*

Josh Moon, a progressive Alabama journalist, replied in a tweet:
"There are literally quotes from KKK rallies, documented in
FBI transcripts from the 1960s, that are close to this. The only
difference is those racists had enough shame to wear hoods."

Breivik's Nordic Blood Fears

Somewhere in a Norwegian prison, where he has lived since
he was convicted of murder, Anders Breivik must be smiling:
The president and prominent figures in the United States
of America—the land of, "Give me . . . your huddled masses
yearning to breathe free"—are espousing the central tenet of a
treatise on white extinction anxiety that the Norwegian spent
years preparing. His position, and Trump's, can be boiled down
to three words: too many foreigners. Breivik blurted those words
to the first police officers who made their way—finally—to Utøya
island. "This is politically motivated," he declared. "The country
is being invaded by foreigners." This is the opening salvo from
Breivik's manifesto:

*As we all know, the root of Europe's problems is the lack
of cultural self-confidence (nationalism). Most people
are still terrified of nationalistic political doctrines,
thinking that if we ever embrace these principles again,*

new "Hitlers" will suddenly pop up and initiate global Armageddon . . . Needless to say, the growing numbers of nationalists in W. Europe are systematically being ridiculed, silenced and persecuted by the current cultural Marxist/multiculturalist political establishments. This has been a continuous ongoing process which started in 1945. This irrational fear of nationalistic doctrines is preventing us from stopping our own national/ cultural suicide as the Islamic colonization is increasing annually. This book presents the only solutions to our current problems.

Like nativists in other European nations, Breivik was mortified that immigrants were bearing more children than native Norwegians. And he saw the diminishment of Nordic blood through race-mixing as a pan-Atlantic crisis:

Within approximately 100-150 years or within 4-5 generations (if the current development is allowed to continue), the Germanic/Nordic race in several countries will be diluted or annihilated to such a degree that there will be no one left with Nordic physical characteristics; blonde hair, blue eyes, high forehead, sturdy cheekbones. As such, the Nordic tribes will become extinct if we do not resist and seize political and military control of our countries. To illustrate the ongoing demographic annihilation of the Nordic peoples: in 1900 there were 50% Nordics in the US (blonde hair, blue eyes). But now,

as a result of primarily non-European immigration, there
was in 2008 ONLY 16%.

Breeding Initiatives

His solution for this hair-color "demographic warfare": production of more babies of Aryan purity to counteract "the rapid extinction of Nordic genotypes." Employing mathematical equations about fertility rates, his manifesto recommends a series of breeding initiatives that recall Margaret Atwood's *The Handmaid's Tale*. A Norwegian "reproduction industry" centered around breeding colonies would incentivize blonde, Amazonian women to reproduce, either naturally or via the outsourcing of sperm and eggs to surrogate mothers in "low-cost countries." Birth control would be carefully restricted by the government and abortion would be illegal. Women would be discouraged from careers, and their education would be limited. ("This will involve certain sexist and discriminating policies," Breivik allows, "but should increase the fertility rate . . .") His ideas spin on and on, including contemplations on the development of artificial wombs that would remove human flesh entirely from the procreative process.

This is not science fiction to Breivik's peer group of proselytizers for eugenics (even if they are savvy enough not to use that loaded word). The urgency of increased Caucasian breeding is a bedrock principle among white supremacists. The subject was on the agenda at the June 2018 "National Solutions Conference" of the white nationalist Council of Conservative

Citizens, held at a Tennessee state park west of Nashville. Among the speakers was Virginia Abernethy, a controversial professor emeritus at Vanderbilt University. A conference summary reported that Abernethy:

> *discussed the declining birth rate among American and European whites and explained how this statistic will determine our continued survival as a race. She suggested some extremely radical measures to encourage a greater live white birth rate, such as subsidies to white couples by wealthy benefactors.*

(The Southern Poverty Law Center says Abernethy "pushes repugnant, race-based politics from behind an academic veneer.")

Oddly, despite his obsession with Norwegian fertility, Breivik had not done his part as a breeder—though he had gotten a nose job to enhance his Aryan credibility. He was 32 years old, prime breeding age, on the date of his massacre, but many of his friends believed he was gay and depressed over repressed sexuality. He mentions homosexuality disapprovingly nearly two dozen times in his manifesto, though he employs the some-of-my-best-friends proviso: "I personally know several gay individuals . . . and I don't have any reservations against them." He was known to wear make-up and suggested that his fellow knights do the same in one of the manifesto's countless trippy tangents. Warning that police "usually 'leak retarded-looking' photos" to the press, he suggested that his imaginary fellow terrorists prepare glam shots:

Use professional makeup artists, and use makeup on both female and male models. Yes, this sounds gay, but looking "attractive" will significantly benefit the impact of our message as it will act as a force multiplier . . . As a Justiciar Knight you will go into history as one of the most influential individuals of your time. So you need to look your absolute best and ensure that you produce quality marketing material prior to operation.

Norwegian Immigration

One might reasonably wonder how Norway became an incubator for a man with off-the-rails recommendations about a blue-eyed genetic resistance, women as breeding slaves, advance preparation of glam shots for would-be killers, and—in another long, chilling section—attacks on European nuclear power plants? This Scandinavian nation seems like a nice place to live. It has one of the world's most stable, productive economies and highest standards of living, and its streets are among the cleanest and its crime rate among the lowest in the world. Norway ranked first among 155 countries in the 2018 United Nations World Happiness Report, based upon such things as the GDP, social support, health, freedom, and the generosity of its people. In a separate ranking, Norway's foreign-born population was ranked third-happiest, behind Finland and Denmark. Breivik, raised by a mentally ill mother and an absentee father, apparently did not inherit this native Norwegian contentment.

About one million of Norway's 5.3 million people live in metropolitan Oslo, Breivik's hometown. Immigration has spiked in Norway since 2000 and grew more acute beginning in 2015, with the European crisis of refugees arriving from Muslim-majority countries. Many of Norway's new arrivals have settled in Oslo, just as immigrants are also attracted to other bigger cities around the world. The total Norwegian immigrant population numbered about 915,000 in 2018, including the Norway-born children of foreign arrivals, according to government statistics. Immigrants accounted for 16.3 percent of the country's and roughly 25 percent of Oslo's population. Although Breivik cited a "Muslim invasion," the new arrivals can hardly be regarded as an Islamic monolith. More than half have come from other European Union countries, about a third from Asia and Turkey, and 15 percent from Africa, the government reported.

Breivik's Right-Wing Ideology

Breivik explains in his manifesto that he self-radicalized about Islam through online contacts with Serbian Christians outraged by the civilized world's reaction to their genocide of Bosnian Muslims. (Using Wikipedia as a primary source, Breivik dedicates scores of numbing manifesto pages to a torturously detailed history of Serbia in a failed attempt to excuse the genocide.) Seeking to place blame, he cites the same short list of ideologies that pop up frequently among his right-wing contemporaries in the U.S. and Europe: political correctness, liberalism (or Marxism), and feminists:

Political correctness now looms over Western European society like a colossus. It has taken over both political wings, left and right. Among so-called Western European "conservative" parties, the actual cultural conservatives are shown the door because being a cultural conservative opposes the very essence of political correctness. It controls the most powerful element in our culture, the media and entertainment industry. It dominates both public and higher education: many a college campus is a small, ivy-covered North Korea. It has even captured the higher clergy in many Christian churches. Anyone in the Establishment who departs from its dictates swiftly ceases to be a member of the Establishment . . . Some people see it as a joke. It is not. It is deadly serious. It seeks to alter virtually all the rules, formal and informal, that govern relations among people and institutions. It wants to change behavior, thought, even the words we use.

As a contrast, he sketched a word portrait of his ideal era, the 1950s, when tongues were unbitten: "In the office, the man might light up a cigarette, drop a reference to the 'little lady,' and say he was happy to see the firm employing some colored folks in important positions." Breivik missed out on that "Mad Men" bonhomie, because he was born in 1979. "Who dares to speak of 'ladies' now?" he asks. Anders Breivik, that's who. A few more excerpts:

ON FEMINISM

Perhaps no aspect of Political Correctness is more prominent in Western European life today than feminist ideology . . . Where do we see radical feminism ascendant? It is on television, where nearly every major offering has a female "power figure" and the plots and characters emphasize inferiority of the male and superiority of the female. It is in the military, where expanding opportunity for women, even in combat positions, has been accompanied by double standards and then lowered standards . . . It is in government-mandated employment preferences and practices that benefit women and use "sexual harassment" charges to keep men in line. It is in colleges where women's gender studies proliferate and "affirmative action" is applied in admissions and employment. It is in other employment, public and private, where in addition to affirmative action, "sensitivity training" is given unprecedented time and attention. It is in public schools, where "self-awareness" and "self-esteem" are increasingly promoted while academic learning declines. And sadly, we see that several European countries allow and fund free distribution of contraceptive pills combined with liberal abortion policies . . . There is no doubt in the media that the "man of today" is expected to be a touchy-feely subspecies who bows to the radical feminist agenda . . . Indeed the feminization of European culture is nearly completed.

ON MUSLIMS

Multiculturalism (cultural Marxism/political correctness), as you might know, is the root cause of the ongoing Islamization of Europe which has resulted in the ongoing Islamic colonization of Europe through demographic warfare (facilitated by our own leaders) . . . Time is of the essence. We have only a few decades to consolidate a sufficient level of resistance before our major cities are completely demographically overwhelmed by Muslims . . . If we had learned from our own history, from our Eastern European brethren, we could have avoided this mess altogether. European demographical studies, especially in the Balkans and elsewhere, confirm that the Global Islamic Ummah has deliberately waged a demographic warfare against Eastern Europe since the fall of the Christian Byzantine Empire . . .

Breivik weighed in on a breathtaking array of topics—recommending, for example, the increased corporal punishment of children "at home and school." He also revealed himself to be an attentive viewer of America's Fox News, which has made bedrock doctrine of the fake-news "issue" of holiday greetings. Breivik huffs:

Celebration of Christmas and Easter is now considered offensive to Muslims so it is now inappropriate to actually say Merry Christmas. Instead we must say, Happy holidays . . . And people still don't get it? It can't be said clearer than this: the Western European cultural Marxist regimes want you to abandon God and the Church . . . Currently, we are embroiled in a bitter spiritual war that will inevitably lead to a physical one. Such vitriol always ends up leading to violence, whether it is a genocidal slaughter, or a civil war—the spiritual war transcends to the physical plane, and God's people are once again embroiled in a bloody battle.

The Merry Christmas/Happy Holiday War? As I suggested, Breivik betrays his madness on nearly every page, including the scores of them devoted to a Q&A interview with himself. ("Q: How would you describe yourself as a person? A: I consider myself to be a laid-back type and quite tolerant on most issues. Due to the fact that I have been exposed to decades of multicultural indoctrination, I feel a need to emphasize that I am not in fact a racist and never have been.") He returns frequently to declarations of open-mindedness, despite a million words of evidence to the contrary. "Loving your extended family/your ethnic group and fighting for ethnic and/or indigenous rights does not make you a racist, quite the opposite in fact," he writes. "It makes you a civil rights activist."

After spending many hours with Breivik's document, I concluded that it was time wasted. We pore over the leavings of killers in hopes of finding some nugget whose careful examination might prevent history from repeating itself, like the wild elephants who scrutinize the bones of fallen members of their species, but I found nothing in this sad, demented man's soul. The Norwegian author Karl Ove Knausgård, who has extensively explored Breivik's life, crimes, and dissertation, writes that there is nothing to be learned from him:

> *He wanted to be seen. That is what drove him, nothing else. Look at me. Look at me. Look at me . . . He is a person filled to the brim with himself. And that is perhaps the most painful thing of all, the realization that this whole gruesome massacre, all those extinguished lives, was the result of a frustrated young man's need for self-representation . . . I do not believe that Breivik himself has anything to teach us . . . Breivik's childhood explains nothing, his character explains nothing, his political ideas explain nothing.*

Breivik relished his look-at-me moment in the spotlight during his criminal trial. He posed making a Nazi salute. He sneered. He smiled. He wept. He proclaimed that he had acted out of "goodness, not evil . . . in self-defense on behalf of my people, my city, my country." But his most cogent message can be found in these six words: "I would have done it again."

Chapter 10.
The Industrial
Revolutionary

Among the broad range of motives for mass killers—from sexual complaints to blatant racism to amorphic juvenile cavils—Anders Breivik's may have been most closely aligned with that of a man who lived like a hermit in a hovel in the Montana woods, nearly 5,000 miles from Oslo. Like Breivik, serial killer Ted Kaczynski killed (and maimed) as part of a whacked-out quest to publicize a personal doctrine that he saw as urgent for the survival of humankind. Kaczynski, once a rising-star mathematician, had grown convinced that technology was destroying us. And like Breivik, he produced a windy manifesto to make his case, whose principal theme was insanity.

For nearly two decades, the inscrutable postal terrorist that federal authorities branded the "Unabomber" had baffled American law enforcers. His nom-de-crime was drawn from his early targets—**UN**iversities and **A**irlines—and his weapon of choice.

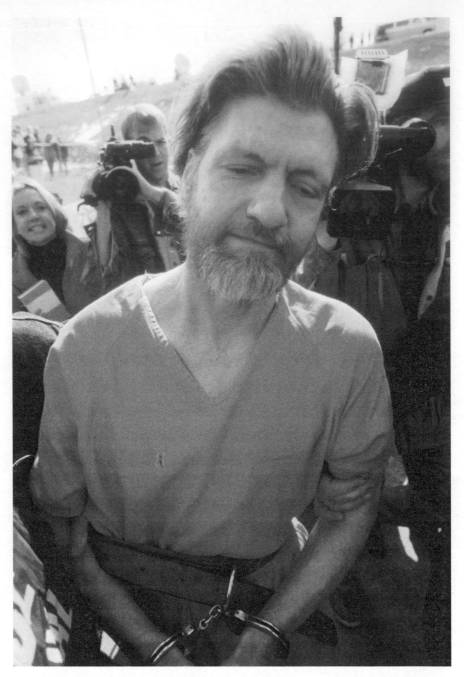

Ted Kaczynski lived in isolation in the wilderness and became convinced technology was destroying humankind. He hit upon an insane way of hammering home his message.

First Bomb-in-a-Box

Kaczynski's curtain-raising explosion, a pipe bomb nestled in a meticulously crafted wooden box, went off on May 25, 1978. The method of delivery was diabolical: He wrapped the box in postal paper and left it in a parking lot at the Chicago campus of the University of Illinois, although his true target was the engineering school at nearby Northwestern University. (He regarded "elite" scientists and engineers as enemies because they promoted technological advances.) Choosing randomly from the Northwestern faculty roster, he selected a young engineering professor there as the return addressee, presupposing that someone would find the package and return it to the sender. His hypothesis was correct.

On that spring day, Professor Buckley Crist received a call from the University of Illinois campus police asking whether he would like his parcel returned. Crist was puzzled. "The person who ostensibly sent that package was me, which was not true," Crist recalled in 2016 on a Northwestern podcast. "My antenna was up. Obviously, something was amiss." The package was delivered by courier, and Crist gingerly used scissors to cut away the paper wrapper, trying to preserve the evidence of what he suspected was an illegal narcotics delivery. Under the paper he found a carved wooden box with a small door inscribed "OPEN." He said that he was spooked by the "stupid little door . . . and I said, 'I'm done.'"

Crist wanted to call in police bomb experts, but a Northwestern campus cop, Terry Marker, opened the box. As he did, it exploded with a deafening report.

Inside was a nine-inch piece of inch-diameter steel pipe packed with explosive powder, rigged to ignite with matchheads when the door was opened. Despite the big bang, the bomb was a dud. The inexperienced bomb-maker had sealed one end of the pipe with a wooden plug instead of a threaded metal cap, so the device lacked the compression to blow the steel into deadly fragments. Marker escaped with a minor hand injury, and university officials and law enforcers mostly shrugged at the incident. It seemed like an anomaly. "They collected all the bits and pieces and dumped it in a trash can," Crist said.

Growing Death Toll

The explosion gained new importance a year later when a second bomb-in-a-box at Northwestern injured a student who opened it. That was followed quickly by two others in the Chicago area—one that was sent to the president of United Airlines, and a second placed in the cargo hold of an American Airlines flight out of Chicago, which smoked but failed to explode. An FBI task force that grew to 100 agents pursued the elusive bomber throughout the 1980s, as a series of explosive devices arrived at universities in Utah, Tennessee, California, and Michigan. After multiple injuries, the Unabomber scored his first fatality in December 1985, when Hugh Scrutton, 38, was killed by a bomb crafted to look like a piece of lumber, which had been left outside RenTech, his computer rental store in Sacramento, California.

After a six-year hiatus from 1987 to 1993, the Unabomber went back to work. The death toll grew to three as he expanded his targets to include computer scientists, geneticists, businessmen, and a lobbyist. Thomas Mosser, an executive with global public relations firm Burson-Marsteller, was killed in 1994 by a bomb delivered to his New Jersey home. Four months later, in April 1995, Gilbert Murray, chief lobbyist for a California timber organization, died when he opened a letter bomb delivered to his Sacramento office.

Turned in by His Brother

After 17 years in the shadows, the Unabomber came into the light. In June 1995, he mailed to *The Washington Post* and *The New York Times* a 35,000-word document—"Industrial Society and Its Future"—about the danger of encroaching technology. He offered a deal: no more violence if his document was published. After a series of meetings between editors and federal officials, the *Post* printed the manifesto as an eight-page supplement on September 19, 1995. A few days later, David Kaczynski, a social worker in Albany, New York, tracked down a copy of the document, motivated by a comment his wife, Linda, had made that summer. "David," she asked, "has it ever occurred to you, even as a remote possibility, that your brother might be the Unabomber?" He later wrote in his memoir:

> *Reading the manifesto on a computer at our local library, I was immobilized by the time I finished the first paragraph. The tone of the opening lines was hauntingly similar to that of Ted's letters condemning our parents, only here the indictment was vastly expanded. On the surface, the phraseology was calm and intellectual, but it barely concealed the author's rage. As much as I*

*wanted to, I couldn't absolutely deny that it might be my
brother's writing.*

David and Linda Kaczynski pored over letters from David's
brother, seven years older than he was, and concluded that the
similarities could not be coincidental. Ted, born in Chicago in
1942, was once a math prodigy who had won a scholarship to
Harvard at age 16. He seemed to be on track to become a leading
academician in his field after earning a Ph.D. from the University
of Michigan and a professorship at Cal-Berkeley, but he walked
away in 1971, eventually retreating to the Montana woods.

A lawyer for David and Linda Kaczynski approached the
FBI, and on April 3, 1996, a phalanx of federal agents roused
Ted Kaczynski, then 53 years old, from his cramped cabin south
of the Montana mountain town of Lincoln. There was no doubt
they had found their man. Kaczynski was a packrat who had
saved copies of every letter he had sent or received, vast stacks
of Unabomber newspaper clippings, and journals that ran into
thousands of pages, with detailed accounts of the planning,
construction, and execution of each bomb.

Investigators learned that Kaczynski had taken macabre
delight in his work. After reading in a San Francisco newspaper
that his first murder victim, computer salesman Scrutton, had
been "blown to bits," Kaczynski wrote in his journal: "Excellent.
Humane way to eliminate somebody. He probably never felt a
thing. $25,000 reward offered. Rather flattering." He had built
his early bombs while living in Chicago, but later he crafted the
explosives in the cabin. Then he took long automobile trips—

often more than 2,000 miles (3,200 km)—to Provo, Utah, or San Francisco to deliver or mail the deadly devices. Charged with multiple felonies, Kaczynski avoided the possibility of capital punishment by pleading guilty to murder and other charges in 1998. He was sent to the federal "supermax" prison in Florence, Colorado, on a life sentence without the possibility of parole.

Anti-Technology Revolution Dreams

Why did the worm turn in the brain of a man regarded as highly intelligent? Like many mass killers, he had grown increasingly paranoid, alienated, and isolated—from his family, professional peers, and, finally, civilization itself. He existed on foraged food in a squalid, cave-like cabin that was just five paces deep and four wide. Living without electricity and plumbing, he spent countless days alone, handcrafting his bombs out of wood and metal. His manifesto makes it clear that the troglodyte lifestyle suited him; he was petrified of modernity and convinced that modern comforts would ultimately deprive him of "control over his own fate," as he wrote. Here is his manifesto's thesis statement:

> The Industrial Revolution and its consequences have been a disaster for the human race. They have greatly increased the life-expectancy of those of us who live in "advanced" countries, but they have destabilized society, have made life unfulfilling, have subjected human beings to indignities, have led to widespread psychological suffering (in the Third World to physical suffering as well) and have inflicted severe damage on the natural

world. The continued development of technology will
worsen the situation.

Like Norway's Breivik, Columbine's Eric Harris and his acolytes,
and the various sex-deprived involuntary celibate killers,
Kaczynski expected to touch off his own mass movement of those
opposed to technology. "We therefore advocate a revolution
against the industrial system," he wrote. "This revolution may
or may not make use of violence." His document also took
a tangential journey into identity politics. Like Breivik and
others, Kaczynski was flummoxed by activist women, liberals,
and other "politically correct types," and declared: "One of the
most widespread manifestations of the craziness of our world
is leftism." By his lights, women, minorities, and the disabled
invited "feelings of inferiority" when they complained of
discrimination. He explained in a revealing passage that veered
far from his central tenets:

> *When someone interprets as derogatory almost anything*
> *that is said about him (or about groups with whom he*
> *identifies) we conclude that he has inferiority feelings*
> *or low self-esteem. This tendency is pronounced among*
> *minority rights activists, whether or not they belong*
> *to the minority groups whose rights they defend. They*
> *are hypersensitive about the words used to designate*
> *minorities and about anything that is said concerning*
> *minorities. The terms "negro," "oriental," "handicapped"*
> *or "chick" for an African, an Asian, a disabled person*

*or a woman originally had no derogatory connotation.
"Broad" and "chick" were merely the feminine equivalents
of "guy," "dude" or "fellow." The negative connotations
have been attached to these terms by the activists
themselves . . .*

*Those who are most sensitive about "politically
incorrect" terminology are not the average black ghetto-
dweller, Asian immigrant, abused woman or disabled
person, but a minority of activists, many of whom do
not even belong to any "oppressed" group but come from
privileged strata of society.*

Yes, this was a man lecturing others about hypersensitivity after
attempting to bring down a commercial airliner because he was
angry about jet noise. He killed a public relations executive because
his firm had the audacity to represent Exxon, the international
oil and gas giant, and murdered the lowly owner of a random
computer store as a totemic representative of technology. And
he maimed or otherwise wounded about a dozen people who
handled package bombs he sent to names picked arbitrarily from
directories, because he believed the world ought to hear him out.
Here are excerpts from that message:

*Technology advances with great rapidity and threatens
freedom at many different points at the same time
(crowding, rules and regulations, increasing dependence
of individuals on large organizations, propaganda and
other psychological techniques, genetic engineering,*

invasion of privacy through surveillance devices and computers, etc.) . . .

"Oh!" say the technophiles, "Science is going to fix all that! We will conquer famine, eliminate psychological suffering, make everybody healthy and happy!" Yeah, sure. That's what they said 200 years ago. The Industrial Revolution was supposed to eliminate poverty, make everybody happy, etc. The actual result has been quite different. The technophiles are hopelessly naive (or self-deceiving) in their understanding of social problems . . .

The revolution must be international and worldwide. It cannot be carried out on a nation-by-nation basis . . .

"We've Had to Kill People"

He mailed or personally delivered 16 bombs as the foreplay of his master plan to present to the world his "crude approximation to the truth." Without the front-page headlines that bombings bring, he said, his message would have been "swamped by the vast volume of material put out by the media." He continued:

If we had never done anything violent and had submitted the present writings to a publisher, they probably would not have been accepted. If they had been accepted and published, they probably would not have attracted many readers, because it's more fun to watch the entertainment put out by the media than to read a sober essay. Even if these writings had had many readers, most of these readers would soon have forgotten what they had read as their minds were flooded by the mass of material to which the media expose them. In order to get our message before the public with some chance of making a lasting impression, we've had to kill people.

That narrative has grown familiar in mass shootings over the years since Ted Kaczynski faded away: He killed because he believed his lunacy demanded the world's undivided attention. More than two decades in prison have not changed that. From behind bars, the senior citizen convict has cranked out a nonstop efflux of book manuscripts, articles, and letters critical of the "global techno-industrial system." His manifesto and two more recent tomes with similar themes are available at Amazon, where his author's page says Kaczynski "has focused his life's work on sounding the alarm about society's paramount problem: the omnipresent, subjugating, and destructive force of technological progress." (He earns nothing from sales, his publishers say.)

His bio glosses over his three murders and the multiple injuries from the helter-skelter bombings. A clutch of disciples cling like dying ivy to Kaczynski and his ideas, and some defend him as a misunderstood genius. After I wrote an article noting the 40th anniversary of Kaczynski's first bomb delivery, one of his minions—a woman employed, oddly enough, by a Canadian technology firm—delivered this whataboutism reply to me: "What's your IQ, bubba-lah, and what is Ted Kaczynski's IQ?

Yeah, that's what I thought." No doubt Ted has a higher IQ. His body count is also higher.

Like most empathy-deprived, sociopathic killers, Kaczynski offers no apologies for destroying innocent lives. In their demented minds, the end justifies the means. In a letter from prison to a love interest who questioned his violence, Kaczynski wrote: "Do I feel that my actions were justified? To that I can give you only a qualified yes."

Chapter 11.
Die Euromörder

Many Americans I speak with are surprised to learn that mass shootings, and especially those at schools, happen with some regularity in other parts of the world. Americans seem to believe that they've cornered the market in gun violence. And why wouldn't they, since Americans possess four out of every ten of the estimated 857 million small firearms owned by private individuals around the globe. On an average day in the U.S., guns are used to kill nearly 100 people and injure twice that many, including homicides, suicides, and accidental shootings. We can't keep track of our own contemporary mass killers, let alone Europe's. According to research by Frederic Lemieux, a criminologist at Georgetown University in Washington, D.C., at least one mass shooting took place in 25 of the world's most prosperous nations from 1983 to 2013. But Lemieux calculated that the U.S. had nearly double the number of cases over those 30 years than all the other 24 countries combined.

The volume of American murder is overwhelming. This has led to an oddly forked, retrospective view of criminals. The legendary (or mythological) crime figures of the Old West are etched in our collective memory. For instance, the name of Billy the Kid, who killed eight or nine people (or perhaps fewer), is widely recognized nearly 150 years after his death. But how many can summon the names of the men who slaughtered 23 in 1991 at a Killeen, Texas, cafeteria; eight at Christmastime 2007 at an Omaha, Nebraska, shopping mall; or even 58—the current record—on October 1, 2017, in Las Vegas? (The answers: George Hennard, Robert Hawkins, and Stephen Paddock.)

The most atrocious international cases have also blipped on the American media radar screens, of course, including two that predated by three years the 1999 Columbine High School massacre. Columbine has become a wellspring and watermark for like-minded young nihilists in Europe, but it was not nearly the first—or the most outrageous. Thomas Watt Hamilton took a position in the international pantheon of infamy on March 13, 1996, when the suicidal Scotsman shot to death 16 children and a teacher at a primary school in Dunblane, northeast of Glasgow. For years, the former Scout leader had been the subject of well-founded gossip that he had taken "moral liberties" with boys, and his life ended with an outrageous act of revenge that was, at its heart, payback for his own failings.

Six weeks later, a mentally challenged Australian named Martin Bryant embarked on a crazed spree shooting in and around a famed Tasmanian tourist attraction, the old prison colony at Port Arthur. Although Bryant's motives remain obscure all these years later, the killer's attorney has suggested that he was at least partially inspired by Dunblane's Hamilton. Bryant, 29, was said to

Nineteen-year-old Martin Bryant had the IQ of an 11-year-old. On the day he killed 35 people and injured another two dozen, he had a meal, set up a video camera on a vacant table, took out an AR15 semi-automatic rifle, and started shooting.

be delighted that he had doubled the Scot's body count, killing 35 and wounding two dozen more. He wanted to one-up Dunblane, and he succeeded. Bryant pleaded guilty to murder and was locked away for life.

School Shootings in Germany

HEINZ SCHMIDT

Eight decades before the atrocities in Scotland and Australia, a troubled German named Heinz Schmidt helped establish his country's reputation for mass violence. A year before the political assassination that triggered World War I, Schmidt marched to battle in his own personal crusade against the Society of Jesus. The Jesuits were the subject of sinister conspiracy theories in Imperial Germany, where many believed that a Vatican cabal played marionettist to a network of puppet governments around the globe. Like many of the believers, Schmidt, a Protestant minister's son, was influenced by Otto von Bismarck. Fearing papal competition, the imperial chancellor imposed a Jesuits Law in 1872, restricting the order's ability to exercise its faith in Germany. The law was intact in some form for 45 years, but Jesuit paranoia festered long after Bismarck was gone.

And it was personified by Heinz Schmidt. Since he was no match for the entire Jesuit cryptocracy, Schmidt chose to attack a proxy: the 1,000 pupils of St. Mary's Catholic School in the north German city of Bremen. He arrived there on June 20, 1913, toting a briefcase sagging with as many as ten handguns and scores of bullets. By that date, Schmidt, aged 30, had meandered further and further off the path of sanity. He had worked as a teacher in Prussia before losing his job after a mental collapse in 1911, but following his treatment at an asylum he was declared cured—although ensuing events would contradict that. Schmidt then turned up in Bremen in December 1912. Described as shy and awkward, he sought several teaching jobs, using forged documents that obscured his biography, which included a diagnosed history of "persecution mania."

Denied a job, he blamed the unseen hand of the Jesuits, and in the spring of 1913 he bought an arsenal of pistols and ammo. His bulk purchases and oddball behavior prompted two separate gun shops to file reports with the police, according to

Der Spiegel, but cursory investigations led nowhere. Meanwhile, Schmidt carped incoherently about Jesuits in his letters home, and his mother rushed to Bremen to urge further psychiatric care. However, he waved her off and was soon marching toward infamy at St. Mary's. Teacher Maria Pohl confronted Schmidt in a school corridor, demanding to know his business, and Schmidt replied with a pistol shot that whizzed past her head. He then fired indiscriminately at a hallway queue of 36 girls, each eight years old or younger. As victims fell, he discarded depleted guns and grabbed replacements from his briefcase. Shrieks echoed through the fortress-like school building, and one girl pleaded: "Uncle, please do not shoot us!"

But Schmidt's only mercy was a lousy aim. A brave unarmed janitor grappled with the intruder, allowing many girls to flee. He was shot through the jaw but survived. Schmidt then moved to a window and fired pot-shots at boys fleeing across a playground outside, hitting five, though none fatally. Next, he was confronted by teacher Hubert Möllmann, who was shot twice but also miraculously survived.

A horde of citizens alerted by the shots then streamed toward the school, and several men, including a carriage-driver armed with a pitchfork, subdued the killer. News reports said the "armed lunatic" was saved from lynching by officers who brandished sabers to hold back the mob. As Schmidt was bum-rushed to jail, the killer bellowed that he had drawn first blood in a war against the Jesuits.

"This may be the beginning," Schmidt cried, "but the end is yet to come!"

Schmidt had killed five girls and wounded 21 other children and adults. He refused to discuss his motive, but his father had died just before the rampage, and *Der Spiegel* said Schmidt had blamed the minister's failing health on the Society of Jesus. "The Jesuits did this," he wrote to his sister. The school shooter was declared insane and confined to a mental hospital for life, which proved to be another 19 years. He died there of tuberculosis in 1932. His rampage was one of the world's earliest mass school shootings, and his targeting of very young children has been compared to Adam Lanza's 2012 assault on first-graders in Connecticut.

ROBERT STEINHÄUSER

Since Schmidt, Germany has stood out in Europe for its dreadful record of school savagery. In 1964, the psychotic (albeit homicidally creative) Walter Seifert, 42, attacked a Catholic school in Cologne, using a lance and an insecticide sprayer converted into a flamethrower to kill eight students and two teachers. Then in 1983, the suicidal Czech refugee Karel Charva killed five in a school shooting near Frankfurt. The rate of school-centered shootings in the country increased after the notorious 1999 school attack in Colorado. Three years later, Germany experienced its own Columbine when Robert Steinhäuser, 19, shot and killed 16 people and himself at a school in Erfurt, from which he had been expelled for issues related to chronic truancy. His primary targets were faculty members, and he sent 12 of them to the hereafter.

Steinhäuser, an avid member of a local gun club, arrived at school on April 26, 2002, armed with a shotgun and a Glock pistol. He donned a black ninja outfit in a restroom, then strode through the building from one classroom to the next, firing at teachers. Sixth-grade teacher Rainier Heise came face-to-face with the killer in a hallway.

"Then all of a sudden he takes off his face mask," Heise told German journalists. "I asked him: 'Robert, what's all this about?'"

When Steinhäuser did not reply, the 60-year-old teacher told him: "If you're going to kill me, look me in the face. Then he looked at me, dropped the gun and said: 'No, Mr. Heise, that's enough for today.'"

Heise locked Steinhäuser in a room, where he killed himself as police closed in. The German left no explanation of his actions, although revenge clearly was a motive. He had also spoken admiringly about the Columbine killers' careful planning, and had told schoolmates that he desired fame. Peter Langman, the American school shooting expert, says Steinhäuser likely was a narcissistic "unprincipled psychopath," described in a psychiatry reference book as someone with "an arrogant sense of self-worth, an indifference to the welfare of others, and a fraudulent social manner." He lived his short life as a con man, like many narcissists. For example, he had managed to hide his school expulsion from his parents for more than a year. He left home every school-day morning for 14 months, as though he were going to classes—including on the last morning of his life.

SEBASTIAN BOSSE

Steinhäuser won a shout-out in the journal of another suicidal German school shooter, Sebastian Bosse, who wounded nine people with gunfire on November 20, 2006, at his former school in Emsdetten. More than a dozen others suffered smoke inhalation injuries from smoke grenades that Bosse employed. There were no fatalities besides Bosse, who killed himself. Of all the European mass shooters since 1999, Bosse aligned himself most closely with the Columbine killers, especially Eric Harris, who—like Bosse—was 18 years old when he committed his assault. Harris was an Adolf Hitler fanboy, and he sprinkled German words and phrases in his journal. This was Bosse's journal entry on September 26, eight weeks before his attack:

> *ERIC HARRIS: Probably the most reasonable boy that a shitty high school can offer . . . pff . . . ERIC HARRIS IS GOD! There is no doubt. It is scary how similar Eric was to me. Sometimes it seems as if I were to live his life again, as if everything would repeat itself. I am not a copy of REB, VoDKa, Steinhäuser, Gill, Kinkel, Weise or anybody else! I am the advancement of REB! I learned from his mistakes, the bombs. I learned from his entire life.*

The entry reveals Bosse as a student of North American mass murderers. REB and VoDKa were the nicknames that Columbiners Harris and Klebold created for themselves. In addition to his fellow German Steinhäuser, he refers to Kimveer Gill, the perpetrator of a 2006 Montreal college shooting; Kip Kinkel, who killed his parents and two others in Oregon in 1998; and Jeffrey Weise, a 2005 Minnesota school shooter. Like Harris and Klebold, Bosse wore a black trench coat during his assault; he named his guns after women; and he complained that he had been picked on relentlessly in school. Also like the Columbine pair, he left an extensive record of the final year of his life as he planned his assault on Geschwister-Scholl-Schule, which he referred to as GSS. Bosse's themes were consistently dark, depressive, and fatalistic, in messages left across a number of platforms—in a journal, on his personal website, in online forums, and in a video. A few excerpts:

> *Why should I do anything? Why should I work? So that I work myself to death in order to retire at 65 and croak 5 years later? . . . I can build a house, have kids and who knows what else. But for what? Eventually, the house is going to be torn down, and the children are also going to die. So tell me what is the meaning of life? There isn't one! . . .*
>
> *All I want now is killing, hurting, and scaring as much people as possible! When you know you can't be happy with your life anymore and the reasons for it pile up day after day, then you have no other choice but to disappear from this life . . .*
>
> *Humans are a sickness. This earth is sick. I can't fucking wait until I can shoot every motherfucking last one of you. Fucking damn bitches . . . They spit on me, they knocked me down, they laughed at me . . .*

Years before celibacy became a defined motive for mass killers, Bosse referred to his kissless status and sexuality in his final journal entry, written the night before his attack. Like Harris and many others, he encouraged "outcasts" to join his club:

> *This is the last evening I will ever see. I should be happy about all this, but somehow I'm not. It's my family . . . They are all good people, and I will hurt them tomorrow. It's sad to know I won't see them again after tomorrow morning. To those I love: I'm very sorry about all this. I never had a girlfriend, I never kissed a girl . . . but wait, there was this wannabe Gothic chick . . . don't like these . . . but I was drunk, so fuck that. I'm not gay! I don't think it's a problem if anyone is lesbian or gay, but I'm not. I like Jill, from Resident Evil Apocalypse and 3 Nemesis! That's why I call my sawed-off .22 "Jill" . . . I hope that other outcasts will be treated better after GSS! And I hope that some of 'em will be like Reb, Vod and Me: A FUCKING HERO!*

Bosse drove to school the next morning in his trench coat, donned a black gas mask, then walked into the building, shooting and throwing smoke grenades at anyone he encountered. He placed several explosives around the building, but they did not detonate. About 20 minutes after the attack began he killed himself with a gunshot to the mouth. He had boobytrapped his own body with explosives, hoping to kill police or rescue workers, but the devices were safely defused. Bosse dreamed of "bodies lying everywhere," but the reality of his attack fell well short of his fantasy, as with many young school shooters. The only body was his own.

TIM KRETSCHMER

A few years later, on March 11, 2009, another gun-obsessed German, Tim Kretschmer, 17, targeted females in an attack on his former school in Winnenden, near Stuttgart. Like his countryman Steinhäuser, he went from classroom to classroom, brandishing a Beretta 9mm pistol that he used with deadly accuracy. At one point, he taunted students hiding beneath their desks, sing-songing: "Are you not all dead yet?" In all, he killed 15 people and himself. Eleven of his victims were female—eight students and three teachers. Kretschmer, a scion of a wealthy family, had revealed fantasies about committing mass murder to a psychiatrist as an adolescent, so the massacre was his dream come true. During the siege, Kretschmer was asked by a hostage why he was killing. He replied: "For fun—because it is fun!" His murderous merrymaking was an inspiration for a more recent German mass shooter with a deep expertise in the deeds of his European antecedents.

DAVID SONBOLY

Like Connecticut's Adam Lanza, David Sonboly had compiled a scrapbook of past cases, and he was particularly awestruck by Kretschmer. Before his own shooting, Sonboly took an eerie, 300-mile (480-km) round trip to Winnenden from his home near Munich to visit the scene of the teen's crimes. (That mass murder tourism recalls Alvaro Castillo, a North Carolina teenager who took a 3,500-mile (5,630-km) round trip to Colorado to visit Columbine High before he shot up his own high school in 2006.) In the summer of 2016, Sonboly, an 18-year-old native-born German of Iranian background, used a Glock 9mm pistol to kill nine people and injure more than 20 others at a McDonald's franchise and shopping mall in Munich's Moosach neighborhood.

Sonboly, raised in a secular Muslim family, had rejected that faith and changed his given name from Ali to David. Despite his dark skin and hair, he considered himself Aryan and admired a right-wing, anti-immigrant German political party, Alternative for Germany. He was also proud that he shared his birthday—April 20—with Adolf Hitler. Sonboly launched his attack on July 22 because it was the fifth anniversary of Anders Breivik's killing spree, who—not for nothing—would have considered Sonboly a stain on Aryan purity. Sonboly, who branded himself with the nickname "Psycho," used a photo of Breivik as his social media profile picture.

After the shooting, classmates commented in an online forum that Sonboly had been bullied at school. "We always mobbed him in school," said one, "and he always told us that he would kill us." Another added: "He said he wanted to carry out a massacre. He said: 'I will kill you all.'"

In Sonboly's room, authorities found a copy of Langman's book *Why Kids Kill: Inside the Minds of School Shooters*, which has turned up in the possessions of a handful of mass killers. Sonboly left a "rambling" manifesto, according to German authorities, but its contents were never made public.

School Shootings in Finland

PEKKA-ERIC AUVINEN

As he made final preparations for his own deadly assault in 2007, yet another 18-year-old European mass murderer, Finland's

Pekka-Eric Auvinen, took the time to add a touch of public relations to the top of the 1,800-word explanation he left behind. He wanted to ensure that the media framed his actions properly by differentiating himself from a *mere* school shooter:

> Attack Type: *Mass murder, political terrorism (although I chose the school as target, my motives for the attack are political and much, much deeper and therefore I don't want this to be called only as "school shooting").*

Auvinen lived in Jokela, a commuter city 30 miles (48 km) north of the capital city of Helsinki, and grew up in "an ordinary family," the local police chief would later say. In the months before his attack, he began parroting non-ordinary ideas, many culled from the Internet. Admiring references to Nazism began showing up in his schoolwork, and in March 2007 he first delineated his plan to commit mass murder in what he called his "Natural Selector" manifesto, borrowing Harris's infamous phrase.

The teenager was granted a pistol permit in October, and a few weeks later, on November 7, he arrived by bicycle at Jokela High School carrying his new pride and joy, a semi-automatic, .22-caliber Sig Sauer Mosquito. He fired 75 shots in just over 20 minutes, killing six students, a nurse, and the principal. Following that, he went into a bathroom and fired a fatal shot at his own head. Auvinen's note included the familiar themes of young mass shooters: his "godlike" superiority and the need for revolution, revenge, and retribution:

What do I hate / What I don't like?

Equality, tolerance, human rights, political correctness, hypocrisy, ignorance, enslaving religions and ideologies, antidepressants, TV soap operas & drama shows, rap music, mass media, censorship, political populists, religious fanatics, moral majority, totalitarianism, consumerism, democracy, pacifism, state mafia, alcoholics, TV commercials, human race.

What do I love / What do I like?

Existentialism, self-awareness, freedom, justice, truth, moral & political philosophy, personal & social psychology, evolution science, political incorrectness, guns, shooting, BDSM, computers, internet, aggressive electronic and industrial rock & metal music, violent movies, FPS—computer games, sarcasm, irony, black humor, macabre art, mass & serial killer cases, natural disasters, eugenics . . .

Today the process of natural selection is totally misguided. It has reversed. . . . I can't say I belong to the same race as the lousy, miserable, arrogant, selfish human race! No! I have evolved one step above! . . .

Majority of people in society are weak-minded and ignorant retards, masses that act like programmed robots and accept voluntarily slavery. But not me! I am self-aware and realize what is going on in society! I have a free mind! And I choose to be free rather than live like a robot or slave. You can say I have a "god complex,"

sure . . . Compared to you retarded masses, I am actually
godlike . . .

Auvinen borrowed many phrases or concepts directly from
Columbiner Harris, including, "Hate: I'm so full of it and I
love it," "Survival of the fittest," and "Humanity is Overrated."
Like many other young mass killers, he insisted that he was not
"insane, crazy, psychopath, criminal or crap like that." Instead,
he suggested he was on a mission to overthrow "corrupted and
totalitarian regimes"—a classic delusion of grandeur, according
to Peter Langman.

"This is not only grandiose, but bears no connection to
what he actually did," Langman writes. "In reality, he shot some
people at his high school. In his mind, he was initiating an action
to topple totalitarian regimes."

The Finland Ministry of Justice produced a 147-page report
about Auvinen that reached a grim conclusion that European
mass shooters are using Columbine as a model:

The perpetrator admired the USA's Columbine school
killings of 1999 and tried to copy several of the details
. . . The material he wrote in his manifesto and diary
was largely copied from the writings of previous school
killers. He was well informed on school killings. At the
time of the Columbine shooting, he was only nine years
old, which suggests that his interest and expertise in the
subject clearly originated from a later period. Another
school killing that interested the perpetrator occurred

at Virginia Tech, again in the USA, in April 2007. By this time, he had already written his first diary entries concerning his plan. The perpetrator familiarized himself with school killings mainly via the Internet, where it was easy for him to see that they had attracted a lot of publicity in traditional media as well.

MATTI SAARI

This chain of deadly lineage across the Atlantic got a new link ten months later, when another Finnish man, 22-year-old Matti Saari, shot up his college culinary class in the small city of Kauhajoki, 200 miles (320 km) northwest of Auvinen's hometown, Jokela. Saari, another depressed misfit, studied Columbine and traveled to the Jokela school, where he took selfies, then on September 23, 2008, he killed ten classmates, then shot himself dead. He left no detailed explanation, but he wrote in a suicide note: "I hate the human race, I hate mankind, I hate the whole world, and I want to kill as many people as possible."

When he carried out the attack, he wore an Eric Harris-branded T-shirt: "Humanity is Overrated."

Chapter 12.
Twinkle Twinkle
Little Gun

The new year was no more than three days old in 1989 as a scruffy Californian named Patrick Purdy sat in a Stockton beer joint, swigging Budweiser and bragging about his super-awesome assault rifle.

Purdy, dressed in military fatigues, stepped away from his barstool and posed in a rifle-assault stance, swinging an imaginary weapon from side to side and trilling his tongue like a machine gun. His audience was the bartender, who must have wondered (a) whether the customer really owned an assault rifle and (b) why someone would sell such a weapon to the sketchy 24-year-old. As he got up to leave, Purdy delivered a parting shot: "You're gonna read about me in the papers."

That soon came to pass. Two weeks later, on Tuesday, January 17, 1989, Purdy and his Norinco 56S assault rifle arrived just before noon, during recess, at Stockton's Cleveland Elementary School. He was outfitted in military regalia for endgame combat against seven-year-olds, and he had inscribed his guns and flak jacket with "Freedom," "Victory" and "Death to the Great Satin." (It was a misspelling; he meant the demon, not the fabric.) A bayonet and a 75-round magazine were affixed to his Norinco, and he carried 150 additional rounds in a pouch.

Purdy slunk toward the playground, slipping through a gap in a fence, stopped 65 paces short of the 300 children at play, leveled his barrel, and blasted away in a swivel motion, just as he had shown the bartender. He fired 66 shots in about 30 seconds, then moved to a second position, where he fired 39 more times. As the doleful wail of sirens approached his position, Purdy drew a 9mm pistol, put the muzzle to his right temple, and killed himself. He left bedlam behind. Five children, ages six to nine, lay dead, and one teacher and 29 other kids were wounded, many of them writhing on the ground in agony.

Purdy had attended Cleveland Elementary as a child, but he felt no particular enmity toward the school. It was the students he detested. Stockton, a Central Valley agricultural hub with a 1989 population of about 210,000 people, had a large Chinese population dating to the mid-19th century gold rush and railroad boom. In the 1980s, Stockton was a welcoming harbor for Southeast Asian refugees, including thousands of Cambodians and Vietnamese "boat people." Many of these kids ended up at Cleveland Elementary to learn how to become Americans, but Purdy thought they were unworthy of his country's welcome, so he delivered a civics lesson on the Second Amendment.

"SCHOOLYARD BLOODBATH," screamed a banner headline in the Reno, Nevada, *Gazette Journal*. "Gunman kills 5,

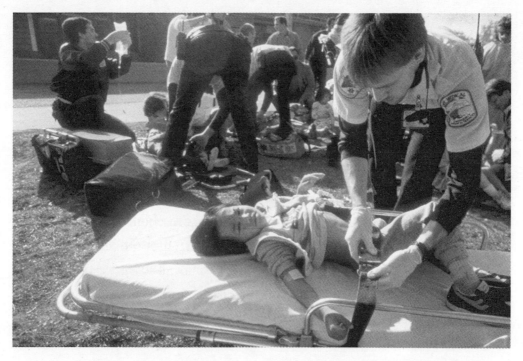

A young girl receives emergency medical treatment after the shooting at Cleveland Elementary School.

wounds 30 in Stockton shocker/Combat-clad drifter shooters 60 rounds, then kills himself."

I visited an online newspaper archive to gauge the scope of news coverage of Purdy's shooting. He won front-page space in papers across the full breadth of the nation, from small towns to big cities—Anniston, Alabama; Asbury Park, New Jersey; Billings, Montana; Chicago, Illinois; Dayton, Ohio; Des Moines, Iowa; Fort Lauderdale, Florida; Jackson, Mississippi; Lafayette, Indiana; Lansing, Michigan; Louisville, Kentucky; Los Angeles, California; Madison, Wisconsin; Pittsburgh, Pennsylvania; Rochester, New York; St. Cloud, Minnesota; Salina, Kansas; Salem, Oregon; Victoria, Texas; and scores of others.

America's Outrage

As we have seen, the escalating trend of mass shootings in the United States began in the 1980s, and that decade had already delivered several horrific case studies in unthinkability. In 1984, James Huberty, a husband and father who was becoming unhinged, stormed into a McDonald's franchise in San Diego, California, and used a shotgun and an Uzi carbine to kill 21 people and wound 19 before he was shot dead by police. Two years later, an angry Edmond, Oklahoma, postal worker named Patrick Sherrill used two semi-automatic pistols to shoot 20 coworkers, killing 14, before committing suicide. (That case gave birth to "going postal," snide shorthand for runaway rage.)

The country was growing accustomed to mass violence, but Stockton seemed to touch a nerve. Nearly all of the dead and wounded were children whose families had fled violence in their homelands and had journeyed 8,000 miles (13,000 km) to the presumed safety of America's Golden State—only to be attacked by a crazed killer. Four of the dead children were Cambodian, one was Vietnamese. Immediately after the shooting, outrage over unencumbered access to guns by people who clearly should not have them played out in American discourse, including letters to newspaper editors from the Atlantic to the Pacific:

New York Times, January 19, 1989
Five children at the Cleveland Elementary School in Stockton, Calif., are dead, and 29 others and a teacher lie wounded. But presumably the National Rifle Association can breathe easily because, after all, Patrick Purdy, a

United States citizen, was not denied the right to bear arms. And we as citizens permit this sort of thing. My question is this: are we all right?—Owen McNamara, Herkimer, New York

Ukiah, California, Daily Journal, March 17, 1989
The gun nuts are coming out of the woodwork after the Stockton school shootings. They hallucinate about being disarmed, losing their free speech and being unable to go "bam, bam, bam, bam, bam, etc." with their AR-47s, Uzis, M-16s and other weapons of war. What does free speech have to do with such maniacal weapons?—W.J. White, Willits, California

Time magazine, a national opinion-leader in that era, scolded: "The easy availability of weapons like this, which have no purpose other than killing human beings, can all too readily turn the delusions of sick gunmen into tragic nightmares."

There were indications that politicians in Washington, widely perceived even then as being in the pocket of gun manufacturers and their chief organizational mouthpiece, the NRA, might be moved to act on gun control. Could Patrick Purdy's assault on pre-adolescent children be a tipping point? Nelson Kempsky, California's chief deputy attorney general, was appointed to lead an investigation into the shooting, and he personally wrote much of the 99-page report. It reached a series of common-sense conclusions that are acutely pertinent today, but Kempsky also showed a degree of empathy for the killer:

The tale of Patrick Purdy's life is not exciting. It is a sad and depressing account of a failed family, of a child without resources who failed to cope with severe stress and lack of affection, and of a human who ended his short life with virtually no ties to the community and society surrounding him. Purdy had lost his struggle with life long before he ended it at the Cleveland School . . . His early years set a pattern of failure and inability to cope which continued without substantial interruption until he died.

Disaffected and Isolated

Kempsky's portrait revealed a disaffected and isolated young man, the template biography that arises in post-mortem profiles of mass shooters in the U.S. and Europe. Purdy was born in 1964 and grew up in Stockton. His namesake father was an Army sergeant discharged for theft and "psychotic instability," and his mother, Kathleen, was submerged in booze and maintained only a "tenuous connection" to her offspring. In the midst of his mother's abusive second marriage, Patrick was removed from her care at age nine—owing to neglect and "intense conflict" between the two—and placed in protective custody.

"Purdy's stepfather physically abused Purdy's mother in his presence, reinforcing his feelings of alienation and helplessness," Kempsky wrote, adding later: "Throughout his life, with justification, he believed he had been abandoned and rejected by his mother."

Mother and son made a final break when he was 13, and a year later he was channeled into rehab, where he was classified as "very drug oriented." At 15 he was homeless and prostituting himself in San Francisco and West Hollywood, California, where he lived for a time with a sugar daddy.

While he was in and out of juvenile detention at age 17, Purdy learned that his father had been struck by a car and killed. Back in Stockton two years later, Purdy had grown up into a slim, 5 ft 10 in ((1.78 m) young man with dirty blond hair. That year he and fellow habitués of a riverside homeless camp were arrested for a purse-snatch robbery. He was locked up for a month, which seemed to inspire an attempt to pull himself together.

After that, he sought counseling for depression, revealing to a shrink: "I have never been able to get along with others or act in a socially acceptable manner." He tried to forge an occupation by training as a welder at Delta Community College, where many of his classmates were Southeast Asian immigrants, completing two courses. But as Kempsky reported: "He was not particularly bright, and he was heavily impaired by constant alcohol and drug use."

Purdy went on the dole in 1984 with a monthly government disability payment pegged to his dependencies. The money funded a new hobby: buying guns. In 1987, he was arrested for shooting at trees in the Eldorado National Forest near Lake Tahoe. He aggravated the problem by resisting arrest, kicking out a police car window. While serving 45 days in jail he acted out on suicidal thoughts expressed during counseling, when he tied a T-shirt into a noose and scratched lacerations into his wrists with his fingernails. He survived but began planning an exit strategy.

Arms-Buying Odyssey

Under the tenets of American gun laws, nothing on Purdy's life résumé or criminal record—not the drug addiction, not the arrests, not the suicidal thoughts—barred him from purchasing deadly firearms. So three months out of jail he used his welfare check to buy a MAC-10 machine pistol, capable of depleting its 32-round magazine in about two seconds. In August 1988, he drove his battered Chevy station wagon 650 miles (1,050 km) north of Stockton to Portland, Oregon, where he lived for two weeks with a maternal aunt. While in Oregon, Purdy plunked down $350 at a gun store called The Trading Post and walked out with his beloved assault rifle, the Norinco 56S. The gun was a Chinese knockoff of the classic Russian AK-47, *Avtomat Kalashnikova*, named for its designer, Mikhail Kalashnikov, a peasant's son with a machinist's soul. The Oregon aunt, spooked by her nephew's gun-collecting habit, ran him off.

"Utterly alienated now and rejected," as Kempsky put it, in the fall of 1988 Purdy embarked on a cross-country odyssey in his Chevy, stopping in Nevada, Tennessee, and Connecticut. He went ammo shopping in Hartford, Connecticut, that December, buying 250 rounds, a 75-round drum magazine, and several 30-round box magazines for his assault rifle. After that, he barreled 3,000 miles (4,800 km) back across the country, returning on December 26 to Stockton, where he checked into the slummy El Rancho Motel, just off the Golden State Highway at the eastern edge of town, where houses yield to farm fields.

On December 28 he bought himself a Christmas gift: a 9mm Taurus pistol. Under state law, he had to wait 15 days before he could pick it up. Purdy stayed busy in the interim. Holed up at the El Rancho, he inscribed his guns and clothing with random words—apparently personal inspirations—including "Victory," "PLO," "Earthman," and "Libya." He then drew a slashed circle over an American flag, and wrote "Humanoids" on a roll of duct tape. Strangely, he decorated his motel room with several dozen plastic toy soldiers. One stood guard atop the TV, another in the mini-fridge, two more in the shower. (His fetish for militaria has been apparent in many contemporary mass shooters, known as pseudocommandos.)

For two weeks before the shooting, he made a series of casing visits to schools in Stockton—on January 5 to Cleveland School, and on January 10 and 12 to Sierra Middle School and the adjacent Lincoln High School, where 700 Cambodians attended special night classes. Staff members at the schools noticed Purdy's odd visits—on January 10, he walked into Sierra and asked a janitor for a dollar—but no one raised a red flag in an era ten years before Columbine. He picked up his new pistol on January 13, then spent time with his half-brother, Albert Gulart Jr., who later admitted that the two had talked many times about shooting a police officer. The men drank beer and admired Purdy's guns—"the best equipped he's ever been," Gulart later said. In the end, Gulart did not join his kin on the school playground—nor did he alert the authorities. An hour before the shooting, Purdy carried his towel-wrapped guns and ammunition to his car.

Kempsky's report recounted the killer's final bon mot:

He chatted briefly with another motel guest who had checked out and was packing his car. The man, who thought Purdy appeared friendly and sober, noticed Purdy putting the wrapped bundles into his car and glanced into Purdy's car, where he saw more covered items on the front and back seats and back floor. The two men joked about the motel's early 11:00 check-out time, which the other guest said was because the motel manager was a "Hindu." Purdy replied, "The damn Hindus and boat people own everything." Those may have been the last words Purdy ever exchanged with anyone. Just an hour later, five small children were dead, thirty schoolmates and a teacher were wounded, and Purdy lay dead of a self-inflicted bullet wound to his head.

Little Has Changed Since Stockton

Kempsky presciently concluded that unfettered access to assault rifles and high-capacity magazines by deranged people like Purdy would inevitably lead to ever-increasing mass shooting casualties. He wrote:

It is not possible to make sense out of an irrational act. We can only look to see if there were reasonable steps which could have been taken to minimize the chances of its occurrence, so those kinds of preventative actions can be taken in the future . . .

Patrick Purdy's murderous rampage could not have happened as it did without the weaponry he was able to purchase quite legally . . . Any significant limitation on the number of bullets he was capable of firing would have saved some children from becoming victims . . . In addition to the prohibition against assault weapons, there is a need for restrictions on high-capacity magazines and drums. Purdy could have done far less damage if he had been restricted to the use of low-capacity clips. He would have had less time to shoot at children . . .

Citizens in a free society have no need for weapons which fire twice a second, nor for 75-round drums of bullets. Restrictions on assault weapons need to be national rather than California only. High-capacity drums and magazines should be prohibited in California and throughout the nation. Conditions of probation restricting possession of firearms should be mandated to be reported to the Department of Justice and entered into the criminal history system. No person barred by a court from possessing a firearm should be permitted to buy one. People who have been confined to a mental health facility because they are a danger to themselves or others should be barred from possessing firearms for a reasonable period of time after their release.

Nearly 30 full years after Kempsky authored that report, I found him living in retirement just 40 miles (65 km) up Interstate 5 from Cleveland School, in a Sacramento suburb. He was surprised but pleased that his report was accessible all these years later. (It is available amid the hundreds of documents at Langman's SchoolShooters.info.) He said:

> *Unfortunately, I could have written the same conclusions today. It sounds like I knew what I was talking about, but it seems so obvious. It proves the adage that if we don't pay attention to history, we are doomed to relive it.*

He agreed that Stockton was a potential tipping point toward gun control.

> *But we ended up going the other way, toward even more ready access and fewer restrictions, and have never gone back. Now I gnash my teeth with each new one, whether it's Colorado, or Connecticut, or wherever. They all feel about the same because we continue to put guns in the hands of people who are clearly mentally ill.*

He explained that this happens because the NRA and the gun manufacturers that profit from unlimited firearms sales operate efficiently in the system of transactional fealty that dominates Congress and U.S. statehouses.

> *Most of the NRA's money comes from the manufacturers, and they are doing a better job of lobbying—meaning*

donating money to politicians, then holding them accountable—than the rest of us. When one side gives money and one side doesn't, rest assured that the policy set by politicians will follow the money.

Modest Gains in U.S. Gun Control

Wendy Cukier, a Canadian academician who founded that country's Coalition for Gun Control after Marc Lépine targeted women in a Montreal mass shooting in 1989, just 11 months after Purdy's, notes the NRA's growing "global influence." The NRA has long had its sights on Canadian gun reforms, instituted after the Montreal massacre but gradually curtailed over the years. As for America, Cukier told me: "Sadly, mass shootings are so common in the USA, each one worse than the last, that people seem to accept them as inevitable and almost 'normal.'"

There have been modest gains in U.S. gun control. An increasing number of Democrat-dominated cities and states have placed checks on gun purchases and ownership. By 2018, more than a dozen states had passed "red flag" gun laws, which allow judges to temporarily ban firearms possession or purchases by people seen as a risk to themselves or others, one of Kempsky's long-ago recommendations.

Perhaps most promisingly, a diverse array of advocacy organizations, scholars, health care concerns, law enforcement groups, and Democratic governors have committed to funding and conducting serious scientific research on the scope, costs, and impact of gun violence. This has been a non-grata subject in American politics since 1996, when Congress—under two-fisted pressure from the gun lobby—effectively ended government gun research by stripping away funding. But the country has shown no political will to implement the sweeping firearms reforms instituted after mass shootings in Scotland, Australia, and Canada.

Some wonder what the point would be, because the U.S. already has more guns than people. Its 328 million residents are estimated to hold an arsenal of some 400 million firearms, including 15 million or more assault rifles, by some counts. (The country accounts for about 40 percent of all firearms in the world, according to the 2017 Small Arms Survey of Geneva, Switzerland.) A few U.S. retailers have ceased selling assault rifles and some accessories, which gun control advocates take as a victory. But while second-hand sales of guns are restricted in some states, including California and Connecticut, the vast majority continue to allow unrestricted transactions between individuals.

A Teacher Copes with the Shooting

In 1989, Julia Schardt, at age 41, was a third-year teacher at Stockton's Cleveland School. She had raised three children before starting her career in the classroom.

> I felt led to become a teacher, and I found it was a good match for me. I particularly enjoyed teaching elementary school, and I loved where I taught . . . Most of my students were born in refugee camps in Thailand or the Philippines. They were brought here by their parents, who were escaping horrific events in Laos and Cambodia. It

*was a very close-knit school because we were aware of
the circumstances of where they came from.*

When I asked Schardt about the arc of her life after the shooting—
how the violent event had changed her—I was surprised when
she said that she and her colleagues had managed to suppress
memories of the shooting, perhaps in survival mode.

*The incident was really something that a lot of us put
aside. For those of us who were teachers at Cleveland
School, there was a lot of clarity at the time, but no place
to put it. There's no kind of scaffold in your life to support
your feelings when something like this happens.*

The violence was intensely personal. One of the five children
killed that day was Schardt's second-grade pupil, Oeun Lim,
eight years old. Schardt was escorted onto the playground to
identify the child's tiny body. Two other kids from her class were
wounded. Yet she carried on.

*It didn't consume me. I wasn't afraid to go to school. It
seemed like such an anomaly. Sure, there are a few things:
I get startled when I hear a car backfire, and I never turn
my back toward the street. But as much as anything, it
settled me into my profession and my career, and maybe
in a way it made me wrap my arms around my career a
little bit more . . . I know it made me really aware of my
responsibility to my students to keep them safe.*

After she retired, Schardt would occasionally socialize with a group of former Cleveland School colleagues. "I don't think the shooting ever came up," she told me. "I think it was put on a back shelf because I don't know what else you can do when you go through something like that."

That changed two years into her retirement, on December 14, 2012, the day that Adam Lanza killed 20 first-graders and six adults at Sandy Hook School in Connecticut. Schardt said that shooting "really brought it back to us." She was moved to become an advocate for gun violence prevention, working with the Stockton chapter of the Brady Campaign to Prevent Gun Violence, a Washington, D.C., nonprofit named for James Brady. Brady was disabled during the 1981 attack on President Ronald Reagan by a gunman with a delusional plan to seize the attention of the actress Jodie Foster.

Schardt's agenda is hardly radical, with many of its bullet points harkening back to the recommendations of Nelson Kempsky's report: federal legislation requiring universal background checks for all gun sales, commercial or private; restoration of the ban on assault rifles and high-capacity magazines that was in effect in the U.S. from 1994 to 2004; stringent "red flag" gun-possession rules for those subjected to court orders of protection for domestic violence.

Frontier Spirit Dominates U.S.

Schardt personifies a trend that took root after Sandy Hook: Since then, most gun reforms have come from the grass roots, not politicians. I asked her to describe her state of mind as the gun issue sits in a 1989 time capsule, with politicians tweeting "thoughts and prayers" after each new shooting while intoning that "now is not the time" to discuss reforms.

> *Pissed off. It's that surface anger. You get to the point where you just get so angry and frustrated. Because you work hours and hours on this issue trying to make a change. And you think you've taken a step forward, and then another shooting happens. And it's the aftermath as much as anything—the reluctance, the resistance of people who know better, or who should know better, who aren't doing anything.*

Rochelle Riley, an African-American columnist for the *Detroit Free Press*, sees racism at work. She wrote:

> *I do not contend that these boys and men shot up schools or a movie theater or a church because they are white. I contend that America continues to allow it because they are white . . . because you can be damn sure that if these shootings had been done by black males, there would be calls to round up all the young black men across the country until we could determine what was wrong with them—or until we, the collective we, which means the white we, felt safe. There would be some change in gun laws. There would be action. And it would be a major, continuing news story rather than one forgotten by Sunday.*

It took Australia 12 days to propose gun law reforms after the 1996 massacre of 35 people in Port Arthur, Tasmania. The conservative government of Prime Minister John Howard, in office just two months, forged bipartisan support for sweeping gun control that included buybacks and amnesty programs which eventually netted more than one million firearms. Stringent new requirements on gun ownership were also imposed. More than two decades along, Australia has had few further random shooting sprees. (Mass violence has not disappeared: The country has had several arson attacks since 2000 with ten or more fatalities, and eight children were lost to a deranged mother's knife attack in 2014.) Prompted by James Holmes's 2012 movie theater massacre in Colorado, Howard wrote a column in Australia's *The Age* suggesting that the U.S. was a gun control lost cause:

> *There is more to this than merely the lobbying strength of the National Rifle Association . . . So deeply embedded is the gun culture of the U.S. that millions of law-abiding Americans truly believe that it is safer to own a gun, based on the chilling logic that because there are so many guns in circulation, one's own weapon is needed for self-protection. To put it another way, the situation is so far gone there can be no turning back.*

Some years ago, Keith Price, a former Texas prison warden, tried to explain why the ways of the Old West—as portrayed by writers like Karl May, Zane Grey, and Louis L'Amour—still hold a grip on America. "The frontier spirit and all its trappings still dominate our culture," Price said. "This explains our love of guns, chivalry, revenge, swift and painful justice, and capital punishment . . . We still view ourselves as the cowboys of our past."

I'm pretty certain that the "cowboy way" is irrelevant to the lifestyle in the big-city American neighborhoods endemically afflicted with gun violence, including impoverished precincts in Chicago, St. Louis, Memphis, Baltimore, and Detroit. But there is no question that the country's long history of liberal access to guns has left the U.S. laden with deadly weapons. The politically untenable confiscation of guns—the longtime NRA bogeyman— is never going to happen in the U.S., and buybacks have not been successful.

Meanwhile, threat-assessment tools designed to identify potential school shooters—one component of a $3 billion school safety industry that has mushroomed in the U.S. since Columbine— are considered ineffective by many experts. And any gun control initiative is politically fraught in many states, even though polls consistently show that Americans favor reforms such as universal background checks before purchases. For example, it seems like simple horse sense that the mentally ill should not be allowed to buy firearms. Among other experts, Lawrence Raifman, a Johns Hopkins University psychologist known for leading seminars entitled "Profiling Mentally Ill Mass Murderers," draws a clear link between firearms access and any number of deranged spree killers.

"More Guns in Schools" Initiative

Yet after a ten-fatality school shooting near Houston in May 2018, Texas Governor Greg Abbott ignited a firestorm by suggesting that the mental well-being of the buyer ought to be considered before a gun sale. Chastened by the gun lobby, he quickly backed down. ("You never get good policy when you base it off of emotion," said C.J. Grisham, leader of the pro-gun Open Carry Texas.) Instead, a new school safety initiative in Texas focuses on "hardening" campuses through increased security and the controversial arming of teachers and other school personnel— known collectively as "guardians." More than a dozen other states, generally those dominated by Republican politics, have considered or enacted similar strategies.

"More guns in schools" has been a template NRA talking point for years, even before a tone-deaf Wayne LaPierre, CEO of the organization since 1991, stood at a press conference a week after 20 first-graders were killed—by guns—at Sandy Hook in Connecticut and said: "Since when did 'gun' automatically become a bad word?"

No Quick Political Solution

Author Malcolm Gladwell, who has studied mass violence, was asked by a reporter in 2018 whether he had "any hope" that supersized shootings would diminish. His reply was:

> No. I mean, it may die out on its own, but nothing we're doing is going to make much difference. It has a life of its own now, and it's fed by social currents that are beyond our control. We're not going to take away the guns, are we? So I'm not terribly optimistic.

The 17 shooting deaths at a Parkland, Florida, high school in February 2018 seemed to move the needle a bit on gun control, due largely to the confrontational advocacy of surviving students there. "I'm seeing some changes, but I don't know how to get out of the politicized morass," Schardt told me. "It's almost as if there's a line drawn, and you either stand on one side or the other . . . It will take a statesman to step forward and be bold." Art Acevedo, the Houston police chief, has chosen a side. He posted this message on Facebook after the school shooting in the Houston exurb:

> *Today I spent the day dealing with another mass shooting of children and a responding police officer who is clinging to life. I'm not ashamed to admit I've shed tears of sadness, pain and anger. I know some have strong feelings about gun rights, but I want you to know I've hit rock bottom, and I am not interested in your views as it pertains to this issue. Please do not post anything about guns aren't the problem and there's little we can do . . .*
>
> *I have never accepted the status-quo in anything I do, and I've never accepted defeat. And I won't do it now . . . The hatred being spewed in our country and the new norms we so-called people of faith are accepting is as much to blame for so much of the violence in our once-pragmatic Nation.*
>
> *This isn't a time for prayers, and study and inaction, it's a time for prayers, action and the asking*

*of God's forgiveness for our inaction (especially the
elected officials that ran to the cameras today, acted in
a solemn manner, called for prayers, and will once again
do absolutely nothing).*

Just days after that Texas shooting, the parents of a prospective
student across the country at an elementary school near Boston
noticed a hand-drawn message affixed to a kindergarten classroom
bulletin board. They snapped a cellphone photo after realizing
that the flier featured Kafkaesque alternative lyrics to the lullaby
"Twinkle, Twinkle, Little Star":

*Lockdown, lockdown, lock the door
Shut the lights off, say no more.*

*Go behind the desk and hide
Wait until it's safe inside.*

*Lockdown, lockdown, it's all done
Now it's time to have some fun!*

The school superintendent, Mary Skipper, acknowledged that
the rhyme might seem "jarring" and "unnatural." But she said a
mindful teacher had created the flier to "help her young students
stay calm and remember the key steps they would need to follow
during a drill or real emergency." Skipper added: "As much
as we would prefer that school lockdowns not be a part of the
educational experience, unfortunately this is the world we live in."

A roadside shrine to those killed at Sandy Hook Elementary School, Connecticut, which raises a question that no one can really answer...

Resources

Borowitz, Albert, *Terrorism for Self-Glorification: The Herostratus Syndrome*, Kent State University Press (2005)

Connell, Raewyn W., *Gender and Power: Society, the Person, and Sexual Politics*, Stanford University Press (1987)

Fox, James Alan, Jack Levin, and Emma E. Fridel, *Extreme Killing: Understanding Serial and Mass Murder*, Sage Publications (4th Edition, 2018)

Hamlett, Laura E., "Common Psycholinguistic Themes in Mass Murder Manifestos," ScholarWorks (2017)

Kalish, Rachel, and Michael Kimmel, "Suicide by Mass Murder: Masculinity, Aggrieved Entitlement, and Rampage School Shootings," *Health Sociology Review* (Volume 19, Issue 4, 2010)

Klebold, Sue, *A Mother's Reckoning: Living in the Aftermath of Tragedy*, Crown (2016)

Knoll, James L., "The 'Pseudocommando' Mass Murderer, Parts I and II," *Journal of the American Academy of Psychiatry and the Law* (March and June 2010)

Krajicek, David J., *Scooped! Media Miss Real Story on Crime While Chasing Sex, Sleaze, and Celebrities*, Columbia University Press (1998)

Langman, Peter, *Why Kids Kill: Inside the Minds of School Shooters*, St. Martin's Press (2009)

Lankford, Adam, *The Myth of Martyrdom: What Really Drives Suicide Bombers, Rampage Shooters, and Other Self-Destructive Killers*, St. Martin's Press (2013)

Lankford, Adam, and Eric Madfis, "Media Coverage of Mass Killers: Content, Consequences, and Solutions," *American Behavioral Scientist* (March 20, 2018)

Larkin, Ralph W., *Comprehending Columbine*, Temple University Press (2007)

Paton, Nathalie, "Expressive Violence: The Performative Effects of Subversive Participatory Media Uses," *ESSACHESS—Journal for Communication Studies* (July 2015)

Thomas, Chris, "First Suicide Note?" *British Medical Journal* (July 1980)

Yardley, Elizabeth, *Social Media Homicide Confessions: Stories of Killers and Their Victims*, Policy Press (2018)

Zernan, John, *Future Primitive and Other Essays*, Autonomedia (1994)

Index

Abbott, Greg 291–2
Abernethy, Virginia 237
Acevedo, Art 293–4
Adkisson, Jim David 182–6
Age, The 290
Akaaboune, Soumaya 138–9
Alexander, Liza 184
Alhadeff, Alyssa 86
Alhadeff, Lori 86
Allen, Hillary 162–3
Andriolo, Karin 25–6
anger of mass killers 40–3, 47–50
Archer, Dale 171
attention-seeking of mass killers 61–90
Auvinen, Pekka-Eric 36, 53–4, 180, 268–72
Baker, Houston A. 129
Banks, Doris 93
Banks, George 91–4
Bath School massacre 97–101
Baumann, Nick 207
Bennett, James Gordon 81
Billingsley, Jody 124
Billy the Kid 258
Binghamton shootings 218
Bismarck, Otto von 260
Bolstad, Orin 14, 15
Borowitz, Albert 77
Bosse, Sebastian 35, 52–3, 68, 263–6
Brady, James 288
Brauchler, George 171–2

Brazill, Nathaniel 68
Breivik, Anders 18, 26, 60, 64, 83–4, 171, 227–30, 234–44, 268
Brown, Carl 197–200
Bruck, David 193
Bryant, Martin 258–9
Buchanan, Patrick 233
Bucqueroux, Bonnie 79
Buruma, Ian 64
Capote, Truman 65
Carneal, Michael 39
Castillo, Alvaro 36, 50–2, 267
Charleston Church shooting 42, 173–7
Charva, Karel 262
Chin, Ong Li 143, 146, 147, 149, 151
Cho, Seung-Hui 13–14, 27, 31, 36–7, 53, 56, 63, 105
Columbine High School shootings 13, 16, 19, 24, 26, 29–30, 33–8, 42–3, 44–5, 71, 179–80, 201, 258
  as inspiration for other shootings 50–60, 71–2, 78–9, 212, 220–1, 263, 264–5, 271–2
  and Trench Coat Mafia 43–4
Comey, James 45, 85
confused journal entries 24
Connell, Raewyn 106–7
contagion of mass shootings 31–2
Council of Conservative Citizens 192–3, 236–7

Crist, Buckley 247–8
Cruz, Nikolas 62, 177–8
Cukier, Wendy 285
Datta, Gargi 160, 161–2
deaths of mass killers 24–7
definitions of mass murder 94–6
Der Spiegel 22
*Diagnostic and Statistical Manual of Mental
    Disorders* 135
Dunblane shootings 258–9
Eastmond, Aalayah 86
Enzensberger, Hans Magnus 22–3, 24
"European Declaration of Independence,
    A" (Breivik) 228–30, 234–6, 237–44
explanations of mass killers 18–22, 23–4,
    29–30, 41–3, 46–50, 103–5, 132–5,
    136–7, 138–9, 140–2, 144–52,
    158–60, 164–9, 176–7, 184–6,
    187–93, 204–8, 223–4, 228–30,
    234–6, 237–44, 249, 251–5, 264–6,
    268, 269–71
Fabrikant, Valery 62
Farook, Syed Rizwan 22
Fenton, Lynne 161, 162, 168
firearm accessibility 16–17
Flanagan, Vester 36, 53, 61
Foster, Jodie 288
Fox, James Alan 20–1, 95–6, 101, 132,
    202
Freud, Sigmund 31
Friedman, Henry J. 25
Fromm, Erich 30
Fryberg, Jaylen 19–20
Gannon, Elizabeth 124
Garbarino, James 135
gender of mass killers 22, 26–7, 106–7
Gender and Power (Connell) 106–7
geography of mass killings 40, 257–8
Ghansah, Rachel Kaadzi 194–5
Giffords, Gabrielle 69, 203–4, 207–8,
    209
Gill, Kimveer 20, 36, 52, 180, 264

Givhan, Walter 232
Gladwell, Malcolm 43, 292
Goethe, Johann Wolfgang von 29
Golden, Andrew 39–40, 219
Gotti, John 64
Grisham, C.J. 292
Gulart, Albert 281
gun control 276–7, 282–6, 288–94
Hamilton, Jessie 103
Hamilton, Thomas Watt 258
Hamlett, Laura E. 18–19
Hammett, Ernest 199
Harper-Mercer, Chris 36, 37–8, 61–2,
    81–2, 83, 128–9, 180
Harris, Eric 13, 24, 26, 29–30, 33–6,
    38–9, 42–3, 44–5, 46–50, 51, 52–3,
    54, 55–6, 57–60, 71, 72, 78, 82, 105,
    124–6, 178, 179–80, 212, 264, 271
Hawkins, Robert 68, 258
Heise, Rainier 263
Hennard, George 27, 258
Herostratus 76–7
Hicks, Jeffrey 14–15
Hitler, Adolf 44–5, 54, 179–80, 264, 268
Holmes, Arlene 156, 157, 162, 171
Holmes, Bob 156
Holmes, James 156–72, 202, 203, 210,
    290
Hone, Philip 80–1
Howard, John 290
Hribal, Alex 35–6, 55–6
Huberty, James 276
Huyck, Emory 98, 100
Immelman, Aubrey 50
In Cold Blood (Capote) 65
incels 109–30, 131–54, 265–6
"Industrial Society and Its Future"
    (Kaczynski) 249–50, 251–5
Ingraham, Laura 233–4
"Insights into the Mind of Madness"
    (Holmes) 164–9
interests of mass killers 81–5

Internet and mass killers 44–5
Jackson, Susie 176
Johnson, Mitchell 39–40, 219
Kaczynski, David 249–50
Kaczynski, Linda 250
Kaczynski, Ted 26, 245–56
Kalish, Rachel 26, 27, 107
Kehoe, Andrew 97–101, 105
Kehoe, Nellie 97–8, 99
Kelley, Devin 156
Kempsky, Nelson 277–9, 280, 282–5, 288
Kimmel, Michael 26, 27
Kinkel, Bill 12, 14–15
Kinkel, Faith 12, 15
Kinkel, Kip 10–13, 14–15, 17–18, 19, 40, 41, 43
Klebold, Dylan 24, 30, 33–4, 38–9, 42–3, 44, 45, 46–50, 52, 53, 55, 59, 71, 72, 78, 179–80
Klebold, Sue 24, 46
Knausgård, Karl Ove 244
Knoll, James 224
Krajicek, David J. 7–8
Kram, Mike 199
Kramer, Geddy 75, 83
Kretschmer, Tim 36, 267
LaDue, John 56
Langman, Peter 8, 24, 32, 36, 40–1, 62, 224, 263, 268
Lankford, Adam 63, 71–3, 87–8, 89–90
Lanza, Adam 36, 60, 63, 69, 87, 202, 203, 210–26, 288
Lanza, Nancy 210, 211, 212, 222
Lanza, Peter 210–11, 222
LaPierre, Wayne 87, 292
Larkin, Ralph W. 59, 78
Las Vegas shootings 30, 60, 201, 219
Lavergne, Gary 65
Lemieux, Frederic 257
Lépine, Marc 112–15, 180, 285
Levin, Jack 95, 96, 101
Lim, Oeun 287

London Morning Herald 80
Loughner, Jared 62–3, 69, 180, 202, 203–10, 217–18
Loukaitis, Barry 39, 43
Lu, Gang 82
Madfis, Eric 73, 87–8
Malik, Tashfeen 22
Manson, Charles 155
Marker, Terry 247–8
Martin, Trayvon 191
Mateen, Omar 69, 70, 201
Mattison, Jack 15
Mazzillo, Sharon 93
McBriar, Jim 6–7
McBride, Karyl 135–6
McKendry, Greg 182
media coverage 79–81, 85–90
mental health of mass killers 41–3, 54–5, 92, 155–72
Michaels-Martinez, Christopher 153
Minassian, Alek 112
Moon, Josh 234
Moser-Sullivan, Veronica 169
Mosser, Thomas 249
Mother Jones 207
Mother's Reckoning, A (Klebold) 46
Murphy, Anne Marie 223
Murray, Gilbert 249
My Twisted World: The Story of Elliot Rodger (Rodger) 131, 152
narcissistic injury of mass killers 131–54
National Rifle Association (NRA) 86–7, 277, 284–5, 290, 292
New York Daily News 94
New York Herald 81
New York Statesman 80
New York Sun 94
New York Times 153–4
New Yorker, The 210
"No Notoriety" media campaign 87–90
notoriety of mass killers 61–90
Obama, Barack 185

Oliveira, Wellington de 53
Orlando nightclub shooting 60, 69, 85, 201
Osborne, Jesse 69
Overmier, Heidi 124
Paddock, Benjamin Hoskins 156
Paddock, Stephen 9, 30, 155–6, 202, 219, 258
Pagourtzis, Dimitrios 50
Parkland school shootings 60, 62, 85–6, 293–4
Paton, Nathalie 58
Pierson, Karl 54–5, 178
Pinckney, Clementa 175, 176
Pittsburgh synagogue shootings 16
Pohl, Maria 261
Porter, Bruce 210
Price, Keith 290–1
Protocols of the Elders of Zion, The 45
Purdy, Kathleen 278–9
Purdy, Patrick 273–84
Putin, Vladimir 14
race of mass killers 22, 91–2
racism of mass killers 126–30, 173–95, 234–44, 289
"radical losers" 22–4
Raifman, Lawrence 291
Ramsay, Evan 39, 43
Ramsland, Katherine 136
Reagan, Ronald 288
Reid, William 161, 172
Reyes, Jose 105–6
Riley, Rochelle 289
Rodger, Elliot 21, 75–6, 111–12, 127–8, 131–53, 180
Rodger, Jazz 138, 145
Rodger, Peter 143–4, 146, 147, 149
Romano, Jonn 82–3
Roof, Dylann 42, 173–7, 187–94, 230–1
Rostand, Jean 63
Roth, Philip 17
Rousseau, Lauren 223

Saari, Matti 36, 272
Sanders, Felicia 176
Sanders, Tywanza 176
Sandy Hook School shootings 31, 60, 69, 87, 210, 222–4, 288, 292
Sarabia, Rafael 9
Sawyer, Jack 68–9
Schardt, Julia 286–9, 293
Schmidt, Heinz 259–62
Scott, Jamie 174
Scrutton, Hugh 248, 250
Seifert, Walter 262
self-radicalization of mass killers 44–5, 191–2, 239–40
Shakespeare, William 77
Shepherd, Polly 176
Sherrill, Patrick 276
Shneidman, Edwin 25
Skipper, Mary 294
Slobodian, Michael 42
Smith, Robert 65–6
Sodini, George 109–11, 115–24, 126–7
Solomon, Andrew 223
Solomon, T.J. 43–4, 46
Sonboly, David 267–8
Sorrows of Young Werther, The (Goethe) 29
Soto, Victoria 223
Speck, Richard 96, 221–2
Spencer, Brenda 66–8
Spencer, Marsha 173
Stair, Randy 36, 56–7, 73–5
Steele, R. Don 116–17, 118
Steinhäuser, Robert 36, 262–3
Stockton school shootings 273–84, 286–8
suicide notes 27–30
suicides of mass killers 25–30
Sutherland Springs church shooting 60
Taxi Driver (film) 118, 119
Temoney, Ashland 173
Teves, Alex 88
Teves, Caren 88

Teves, Tom 88
Thatcher, Margaret 77
Thomas, Chris 28
Tierny, Bryce 207
Tillman, Ben 231–2
Time (magazine) 277
toxic masculinities 26–7, 57–60, 106–7,
    109–30, 131–54, 241, 265–6
Trench Coat Mafia 43–4
Trump, Donald 40, 232, 234
Tully, Andrew 91
Twigg, Gilbert 101–4, 105
Unabomber 26, 245–56
Unruh, Howard 96–7
Utøya shootings 227–8
Valenti, Jessica 153–4

Virginia Tech shootings 13–14, 27, 31,
    36–7, 53, 60, 63, 105, 201
Visiedo, Octavio 197–8
Wainger, Robert 198–9
Weise, Jeffrey 36, 178–9, 180–2, 264
Whitman, Charles 64–5, 219–20
Wight, John 80
Wind, Alex 86
Wong, Jiverly 218
Woo Bum-kon 60
Woodham, Luke 39, 41–2, 43, 105
Wurst, Andrew 40
Yardley, Elizabeth 17, 95
Ybarra, Aaron 36, 56
Zerzann, John 214–16
Zimmerman, George 191

Picture Credits